PRIMARY SCHOOL CURRICULUM

PRIMARY SCHOOL CURRICULUM

Edited by

B.V. VERGHESE

ANMOL PUBLICATIONS PVT. LTD.

NEW DELHI - 110 002 (INDIA)

ANMOL PUBLICATIONS PVT. LTD.
4374/4B, Ansari Road, Daryaganj
New Delhi - 110 002
Ph.: 23261597, 23278000
Visit us at: www.anmolpublications.com

Primary School Curriculum

ISBN 81-261-1047-3

PRINTED IN INDIA

Published by J.L. Kumar for Anmol Publications Pvt. Ltd., New Delhi - 110 002 and Printed at Mehra Offset Press, Delhi.

CONTENTS

PREFACE

For laying solid educational foundation—primary schools have to bear great responsibility. Hence framing curriculum counts most in educational planning.

This book consists of some important topics containing highly researched and tested material on primary school curriculum. The information is gathered from various authoritative sources. Topics like—what is curriculum change?, learning experiences of 13-years-olds, curriculum change as an aspect of cultural change, curriculum improvement programs, curriculum improvement through self-evaluation, organising a professional development day, the history in the curriculum, approach to physical education, the geography in the primary school, design technology in the primary years, computers in the curriculum, art in the curriculum, the music curriculum, religious education today etc. are given elaborate and methodical treatment.

I am grateful to all the scholars whose writings and fruits of painstaking research are cited or substantially made use of in this book. I am also thankful to all my friends and colleagues who have assisted me while preparing the manuscript. Last but not the least, I am grateful to Mr. J.L. Kumar, Managing Director, Anmol Publications Pvt. Ltd., New Delhi for undertaking the publication of this work.

Students, teachers and researchers besides the policy planners and educationists in the field will find this book of utmost use.

—**B.V. Verghese**

PREFACE

1

WHAT IS CURRICULUM CHANGE ?

In his influential work *Management Teams: Why they Succeed or Fail,* Meridith Belbin shows that a successful team needs people with skills, knowledge, aptitudes, interests and personalities which interlock to make a workable organisation. There is also a need for leadership to create a shared sense of purpose, and give direction to the team. These leadership functions in primary schools have increasingly been shared with class teachers through the policy of curriculum coordination. In 1978 the DES survey *Primary Education in England* showed the many ways in which posts of responsibility were being used in primary schools to improve the consistency of work in a number of subject areas, particularly in language and mathematics.

The value of delegating curriculum responsibility in all subjects has been increasingly recognised. Curriculum consultants with specialist expertise have become curriculum coordinators with a managerial role.

Milk Harrison and Steve Gill, in their book *Primary School Management* argue that the degree to which any particular primary school has developed such policies may be indicated by:

- the nature of the decision curriculum coordinators feel able to make without recourse to the Headteacher;
- the understanding of the role shown by the person or persons to whom each coordinator is responsible and the mechanisms by which their work is monitored;
- the degree of consideration of personal needs and circumstances shown in the choice and handling of coordinators;

— the strength of the structures of organisation which support coordinators (e.g. class release time, training);

— whether coordinators are respected as models of good practice in their specialist areas. Does the headteacher act as a good working model for the relationships which coordinators are encouraged to develop with other teachers?;

— the ways in which coordinators are enabled to learn personnel management skills from each other;

— the degree to which coordinators work in harmony with the school's stated aims.

In primary schools responsibility for the work of each individual class in effectively devolved to the class teacher. Whether this state of affairs leads to independence or interdependence will depend on the school's management structure, the level of active management and the skills of the school's curriculum coordinators.

WHAT HELPS A CURRICULUM COORDINATOR TO BE EFFECTIVE?

All the staff need a clear understanding of the role curriculum coordinators are expected to play within a team of professionals. In *The Developing School* Peter Holly and Geoff Southworth discuss several whole-school concerns which impinge on the effectiveness of subject coordinators. Some of the main issues are expanded below.

A Collaborative Atmosphere

Teachers who are receptive to a collaborative approach grow to respect and acknowledge curriculum expertise from within their own ranks. Only with such an ethos can agreement be reached about where classroom autonomy ends and curricular responsibility begins. This is an issue which will vary widely from school to school, but should ever never vary from class to class within one school.

The value placed on reviews and evaluations of aspects of a teacher's work down by peers (rather than the headteacher), is highly significant. It will also be an important indicator of the school readiness for devolved curriculum responsibility.

A collaborative atmosphere can be maintained only where changes introduced are consistently seen to benefit children rather than merely the reputation of the initiator.

An Enabling and Supportive Structure

In school where job descriptions are highly prescriptive, there is little room for individual enterprise and initiative. Job specifications need to show that the school has different expectations of a newly appointed coordinator than from one who has in a post for some time.

The willingness of teachers to accept advice depends on their perception of a curriculum coordinator's ability in the classroom. Teacher will also make judgements as to the value of the advice based on the coordinator's range of experience, ability to organise resources, knowledge of the subject and range of interpersonal skills. As coordinators become more confident in their middle-management role, arguing changes and making principled educational judgements, headteachers must accept that their own views will be challenged more frequently. Headteacher who consider this as a challenge to their personal authority will undermine the confidence of coordinators and discourage them from accepting greater managerial involvement.

Managerial responsibility and support for the coordinators must be made explicit. Who is to monitor their work as managers and offer guidance at critical times?

School Time Budgeted with the Creation of an Effective Coordination Policy as a Priority

— Time available for curriculum coordinators to do paperwork will affect the degree of consultation possible and hence its quality.

— Time for coordinators to work alongside teachers in their classrooms will be necessary in order to change practice.

— Time to allow curriculum coordinators to see teaching and learning in unfamiliar parts of the school will be required for staff development.

Measures taken to overcome Role Ambivalence

Primary subject coordinators have often proved reluctant to direct colleagues and enforce ideas. Many teachers see their coordinating role restricted to writing paper policies and offering tips. Traditionally, primary teachers do not offer comment on colleagues' teaching styles, approaches and lesson plans, or act as critical friends. Those teachers selected as coordinators need to be helped, through training, to behave more assertively. A whole-school commitment to raising standards by improving personal teaching performance helps acceptance.

Availability of Appropriate INSET

The school has actively to promote acceptance that the nature of this devolved responsibility implies emphasis upon managerial skill as well as upon curriculum expertise. Thus teachers selected to become curriculum coordinators will need to develop skills in areas such as the implementation of change, curriculum planning, evaluation and school development, in addition to attending subject based courses. There is also a need to help coordinators develop interpersonal skills.

A Headteacher who gives Conspicuous Support

Success is greater where headteachers and the senior management team actively support the work of their coordinators. This may involve showing respect for local knowledge, giving additional resources when needed and managing information.

Coordinators who are asked for regular reports on their work are likely to feel that what they are doing is important.

Precautions against an Unbalanced Curriculum Focus

There is a danger that the relative strengths of curriculum coordinators may determine the priority given to particular subjects in classrooms. It may also be true that more articulate and forceful coordinators will secure more resources for their subject to the detriment of others.

In addition, if the only attention given to the curriculum is through curriculum coordinators, then subject-based thinking will dominate curriculum development. Emphasis on equal opportunities, IT and other cross curricular themes, will be weakened unless responsibility for these themes is also included in the school's policy.

Is sufficient coverage currently give to *Health Education, The European Dimension, The World of Work* in your school?

A PERSONAL STRATEGY FOR COORDINATORS

The circumstances in which curriculum coordinators find themselves will affect the way in which they can carry out their work and influence others. If you are the coordinator, by considering your actions carefully you can determine the most appropriate way to ensure progress. In *Primary School Management* Mike Harrison and Steve Gill discuss ways that both newly appointed coordinators and those who have been in a post for some time might fulfil their roles:

Arrange to go into other teachers' classrooms to work with them, if possible

You will need to consider the reasons to give teachers for your presence. Are you there as a critical friend; to give an example of good practice in your subject; to focus on an area the teacher has identified; to discover the quality of the teacher's work in your area or to give advice?

To whom should you report what you find in other teachers' classrooms? Is this information for your headteacher, deputy, the governors, senior management team or the class teacher only? Is the decision yours?

Try to develop the necessary interpersonal skills to carry out your coordination roles successfully

Do you have any responsibility to help others to gain these skills? Can you learn from them mistakes and skills of others? Can you help others learn? Are you able to take advantage of management courses as well as those for your particular curriculum area?

Understand the extent of your responsibilities and where they fit into the management structure of the school

You will be carrying out a delegated responsibility on behalf of the headteacher. Can you establish with him or her agreed terms of reference? Where is the dividing line between a class teacher's autonomy and your responsibility? Can you persuade your headteacher to play an active role in defining these boundaries? Make sure that you recognise the school's stated central purpose and aims in the work you do and the changes you are trying to effect.

Ask to control and account for a budget to support your area

You will then be able to buy and use resources without continual recourse to your headteacher. Arrange to find a method of gaining agreement amongst the staff for the use of money in your area.

after Harrison & Gill *Primary School Management* (p. 37) 1992.

MAKING CHANGE HAPPEN

The task is not impossible. Most teachers do want to improve their practice — that is, they want to see the children in their care develop and to teach as effectively as possible.

Since the introduction of the National Curriculum, teachers have made many changes. Unfortunately this has led to some reinforcement of the idea that making change is always personally stressful, usually unproductive and that it always results in an increased workload.

Change is an interesting area of human experience. Attitudes to it tend to be self perpetuating. The individual who dislikes change almost always will have difficulty with change and will rarely be totally positive about its results.

The attitude of the participants seems to be the most influential factor in its successful implementation. Coordinators therefore need to persuade, cajole and effect the attitude of staff toward.

1. The need for change
2. The focus of the change (the curricular area)
3. The change process itself.

The options and strategies outlined will therefore focus not on the content of what is to be changed (these will be detailed in later chapters), but on the process and personal considerations involved when coordinators seek to influence the teaching behaviour of others.

Change is never achieved solely as the result of a management plan, government legislation or incidental INSET. In *Making School-Centred INSET Work,* Patrick Easen comments,

'One difficulty about in-service programmes... concerns who is defining the needs for whom. There is a conventional wisdom which sees in-service work as being designed by 'task analysis' and 'needs assessment'. In other words, the task to be accomplished is analyzed in terms of specific behaviours to be acquired.'

Successful change only occurs when teachers believe in the need for it, know where it is going, are committed to it and have some ownership of it.

As a coordinator your first considerations must be:

— How much do you know about the past and present situation and the opinions of the teachers with whom you will be working?

— How clear are you about the change you require?

— What will you be satisfied with?

— Are you willing to be fully committed to and involved with colleagues?

— Are you prepared to make the change?

To promote curricular change coordinators need to develop the key personal skills:

— to act consistently;

— to maintain hope, belief and optimism;

— to want success (although not necessarily public approval);

— to be willing to task calculated risks and accept the consequences;

— to develop a capacity to accept, deal with and use conflict constructively;

— to learn to use a soft voice and low key manner;

— to develop self awareness;

— to cultivate a tolerance of ambiguity and complexity;

— to avoid viewing issues as simply black and white;

— to become an active listener.

adapted from Everard and Morris (1985)

This process may take several months, but it is likely to take much longer. The change process may develop its own momentum and may keep going, although it is more likely to require continual re-emphasise. Coordinators must accept the teachers' initial enthusiasm may be short-lived when they discover the full implications of the change.

It will be useful to identify stages in the progression towards and through the change.

Assess the current situation.

Build the need.

Construct a plan of action.

Do it.

Evaluate what you have done.

Although not quite as easy as ABC each stage and appropriate strategies are considered below.

ASSESS THE CURRENT SITUATION IN YOUR SCHOOL

It is important for you to know the school's position and what factors will influence it from the outside. You will need to be open about what you are doing and to bevaer of raising the profile of this curriculum area too high too soon. We all react badly to having issues forced upon us.

Gather Information

Find out the quality and extent of children's work in this curriculum area. Which classes appear to door well? Does if feature prominently in work labelled under another subject? Identify where teachers place it in their curriculum planning forecasts.

Find Evidence

Consider if the work displayed around the school give an accurate reflection of children's work in your curriculum area. Take note if there is evidence in class assemblies or similar events. Talk to the headteacher at an early stage to determine their attitude. Examine school documentation of all kinds. Is this area referred to?

Ask Questions

— Listen if colleagues talk about work in your area.

— Will they talk to you about it? (You may already know the answer to this.)

— Find out whether there have been previous initiatives.

— How have colleagues responded to change in the past?

Consider Outside Influences

Make sure that if there is advice from the SCAA or DFE that you read it? Make contact with a local advisor, advisory teacher, school, college or university where advice may be available. Take note of any courses which might help you or your colleagues.

Enquire about any national association for teachers of your subject. Do they have a primary section? Do they have local meetings?

How does the local community fit in? Are there people within your community with interest or expertise?

Parents are bound to be interested to some point. How will they hear about the changes you propose? Make sure that you lay plans to manage this information. What involvement of parents might be considered?

BUILD THE NEED

Establish some kind of file where you keep:

— your note

— relevant documents

— perhaps a diary.

This will help you to show development and progress over time and to demonstrate your success.

Talk to the headteacher in order to:

— discover the headteacher's thoughts and commitment to this area;

— determine current priority within the school development plan;

— establish a professional dialogue between you and the headteacher;

— register your interest and commitment;

— negotiate the next step;

— emphasise the need;

— formulate a rationale and targets for your work.

It will also be helpful to rehearse your thoughts and to think about possible pitfalls. These may be presented to you in an attempt to divert you or hinder your progress by any member of staff. Such blocking tactics may be:

— *'the staff have had too much thrown at them recently'*
— *'we've not got the time'*
— *'we lack the resources'*
— *'Mrs. Green tried this some years ago and it didn't work then'*
— *'do you do this yourself?'*
— *'I tried this for a week and stopped because...'*
— *'our children can't cope with...'*
— *'we've got this in hand already, don't you bother to stir up...'*

In order to deal with these tactics you must be clear about why you are promoting the development or change. Your arguments need to be reasonable and practical:

— Show positive results through your own practice;
— Make sure you can spell out how it will benefit the children;
— Identify work already going on in many classrooms;
— Demonstrate how it will support other areas of the curriculum;
— Explain that it is a legal requirement.

It is important to be specific. Some examples that you may use are:

— *'The lower juniors already do this and it is important to start it early and to develop skills.'*
— *'This allows maths skills and understanding to be practically used.'*
— *'History and science can be developed together when we look at houses of long ago.'*
— *'Children designing in art and craft are also likely to be doing what is required in technology.'*

So far you have been gathering information. You are now ready to draw up your plan of action.

CONSTRUCT A PLAN OF ACTION

It is important that you start to think in terms of a plan of action. This is not a blueprint to be followed by the letter but an agenda which takes account of constraints on development and is realistic about time required for stages of implementation. It will require constant reappraisal.

In order to write this plan write a statement which will act as an aim. It may help you to state the aim in one simple sentence.

For those unfamiliar with this process, a tip is to write down all the relevant words and phrases then try to pare them down to one statement. The next step will be to jot down lots of ways that your aims might be realised. Divide up your list and say which can realistically be achieved, tackled or addressed in the long, medium or short term (you can decide what is meant by short term). This should put you in a position to make some clear statements of intent and a possible order in which to tackle them. This has to be seen as a working agenda and can only be presented as your personal thinking so far. In later stages you will allow others to influence you thinking and the course of events. This mechanism may enable you to hand over ownership of the process to your colleagues.

So far we have described a simple plan of action. Firstly we establish where we are, next determine where we want to be and then we work out a possible route from the former to the latter, recognising that ultimately we may take another route.

Example of Aims for Curriculum Coordinators:

— To get every teacher to include the appropriate use of computers to support class topics;

— To encourage the inclusion of dance within a balanced programme of study for every class;

— Implementation of the school's history policy as a meaningfully integrated part of the curriculum, starting from the children's own experiences;

— Development of simple technological activities now going on in school to include the statutory order for technology and to capitalise on cross-curricular links.

DOING IT

Who can help us? How can we help ourselves? How will we know when we get there?

1. What are we now?
2. Where do we want to get to?
3. How will we get there?

These are central questions that require answers.

Write a Statement of Intent with Colleagues

This will remind you of your aims even when you are absorbed by local difficulties. Stating your aims your intentions in black and white will have an effect. The processing of writing will act as a catalyst.

It will also mean that when views do come out into the open, some may be critical, so be prepared. It may be profitable to refer to it as a draft statement.

Invite Outsiders in

Outsiders can have a range of effects.

They can:

— present new ideas;

— absorb colleagues' hostility;

— say things you might not dare to say;

— clearly state the need;

— provide a more objective view.

Unfortunately they may also:

— steer teachers in an unpredicted direction;

— stir up hornets' nests;

— not be credible to your teachers.

It is important that outsiders have something to offer, are credible and are prepared to listen to you and your colleagues. Talk to people you know and respect professionally. Who do they recommend?

Visit a Local School

This might be a visit for you, you and your headteacher or the whole staff. Choose the school carefully. Don't go somewhere which is too close as there are often petty rivalries between local schools. Avoid authority show-schools, it is easy for teachers to resent other teachers who have already resolved their problems. The best school to visit is one where the corresponding coordinator is like-minded and where they fact challenges of a similar order such as few resources, lack of expertise, lack of confidence. During the visit focus your attention on one or two aspects, as well as getting an overall impression.

Use 'Ghosts'

A 'ghost' is a person, body or event outside the school, the requirements of which may be cited as a need to make a particular change (the government, the LEA, a local initiative). Beware of overplaying this strategy. So many people use it, teachers are good at sidestepping this one!

Run a Series of Staff Meetings and/or a Professional Development Day

Advice is given in the next chapter about organising specific events. It is likely that such meetings will be the core of any discussion that your teachers are involved in, particularly in the early stages. They must be planned with care — one successful one is far better than a series which leads nowhere.

Use the School Council's GRIDS System

Guidelines for the *Review and Internal Development of Schools* (GRIDS for short), use a whole-school approach to engage all the staff through a five state process where:

1. staff are encourage to consider curricular and non-curricular aspects of school life and the appropriateness of the GRIDS evaluation method;
2. areas of specific review are agreed and priorities set;
3. present positions are determined and evaluated with recommendations;
4. plans are laid for development, needs of staff are determined, action is taken and that action evaluated;

5. an overall review cycle is set up.

Build From Existing Strengths

Find out what individual strengths there are amongst the staff. This is where we ask children to start from. It is reasonable that we should display this good practice in a management situation.

Tackle Classroom Management Issues early on

There are few issues to do with the curriculum which do not impinge on classroom management. This leads most frequently to the failure of change in the classroom. Teachers are often wary of discussing their classroom management. They may feel that they will be judged as formal or inflexible. Avoid descriptions which emphasise polarities, such as — structured or unstructured, didactic or discovery methods, child-led or teacher-led. These do not serve to unit colleagues. The most realistic start might be to say that you recognise that there are a multiplicity of approaches and professionals should select those which are most appropriate. However we have to make clear to the teachers that no-one has the right to be an island because children pass from one class to another. Consistency and continuity demand some common practice, hence flexibility and cooperation are needed.

Use Children and their Learning as a Constant Reference Point

All teachers have children's learning as a common goal, so use it. Ask colleagues how their children might react to an activity. If you know the children it may be useful to refer to individuals. Ask colleagues about the range of abilities in their group. Encourage teachers to bring children's work along to meetings.

Use Literacy and Numeracy as Common Reference Points

Again these aspects of the curriculum are common to all age groups and teachers have a real desire to develop them. If you subject enhances children's learning in these areas it is important to stress them and to use them. In fact they could be the focus of development in a foundation area.

Provide Advice as Coordinator

It may not be possible for you to answer all the questions from teachers in relation to your curriculum area but it is important that answers are found. You may be able to refer to resources or to other people or places where the issue can be addressed. The research phase outlined earlier will be invaluable to you as you build up a network of information, contracts, friends, and references.

Provided a Resource Base

This is something that you can develop from day one. You may have little in the way of funds but invariably you can make a start by establishing a resource base for teachers and children. This will have several effects. It will help to establish that you are the coordinator, that the job needs doing and that it has direct benefits to your teacher colleagues.

Set Attainable Goals

Small steps, like asking teachers to use a new simple resources, may lead through success to larger strides. Teachers who experience failure are sometimes very hard to re-motivate.

Be a Professional Friend

Strong a professional relationships with colleagues may help or hinder your initiatives. You must strive for a professional relationship. This means you can trust one another. Teaching and learning are the focus of relationships. In order to build such a relationship you may have to demonstrate your skills and admit to one or two personal weaknesses.

Avoid Bottomless Pits

Some colleagues will absorb all your energy and give nothing in return. You have limited time and cannot effort to devote it to lost cause. These teachers may have to be worked around. In time they might approach you in order not to be left out of the exciting developments undertaken by their colleagues.

This is not an excuse however to ignore those teachers who might well have doubts, those who feel insecure with the changes you are instigating and those who are not immediate converts. These teachers are your challenge, the reason you have the post of coordinator. It is by the changes in their behaviour that you will be able to measure your progress.

Act Like a Swan

In the most difficult times swans appear clam and tranquil on the surface even if actually padding like mad underneath.

EVALUATE WHAT YOU HAVE DONE

Evaluation has to be an ongoing process, rather than something which we do later to determine our level of success. Evaluation needs to be inherent in the process rather than merely a step in the management plan. Periodic reviews where we assess, evaluate, refocus and re-emphasise, are part of that process but not the whole story. Be sure to act on the result of the evaluation. Teachers will value the process if it leads to something worthwhile but are naturally wary of anything which seems like timewasting.

There are a number of prerequisites for evaluation. It is essential that you and you colleagues are clear about your aims. Joseph Novak and Bob Gowin in *Learning How to Learn* remind us that in order to evaluate, we must first know what we mean by value. What positive outcomes did we seek to achieve? You will be able to assess this better if your school has a clear overall statement of purpose such as a mission statement or published aims. In turn, the aims relating to your subject area will correlate with those of your school as a whole and will thereby be more easily understood.

Approaches to Evaluation

How do you do it? The GRIDS approach (mentioned above) may be used as an example of an attempt to create a compromise between the aspirations of individuals and the need to make progress as a group.

David Playfoot et al. in *The Primary School Management Book* list six other approaches:

— structured staff discussion;

— staff interviews;

— work shadowing;

— paired observation;

— interest group sessions;

— snowball sessions;

— formulation of performance indicators.

These, they suggest, might be used within the stages in GRIDS or in a process like GRIDS.

The following strategies will assist the smooth running of any evaluation.

Question and evaluation

Why, when and what do you wise to evaluate? Who do you want to be involved?

Feedback

Be clear about the form of the feedback from evaluation. It must be accurate and fairly stated so that staff can determine what action to take .

Realism

Be realistic and honest at all times. It is worth waiting a little longer in order to carry the whole team with you. Do not attempt to force issues, overstate your case, or allow your enthusiasm to cause you to mislead your colleagues.

Balance

Seek a balanced picture where you can identify both positive and negative effect and where success and degree of success (the word failure can usually be avoided) can be reported.

Progressively focus your attention

As change takes time, so the context will alter. Some staff will be promoted and others will retire, new teachers will arrive, roles responsibilities and priorities will change and government initiatives will come and then be superseded. Don't allow yourself to become frustrated by the fact that your targets do not stand still. Expect redefinition of your goals, plan for the possibility of new initiatives and were possible, use them to your advantage.

Use a mix of strategies and approaches

No use method will do. Variety will allow everyone to contribute more fully.

Manage the evaluation

Sensitivity is required. Your management of the evaluation process should be deliberate. You must seek meaningful and worthwhile evaluation but always recognise that the school is run by human beings with frailties and the capacity to misjudge situations.

SKILLS FOR SUCCESSFUL COORDINATION

In addition to whole-school prerequisites, personal skills and attitudes will greatly influence the achievements of the coordinator. Management at all levels is predominantly about interpersonal relationships. Thus curriculum coordinators need to consider the range of their interpersonal skills and how to get their messages across.

Effective Communication

Some teachers may find that their opportunities to influence colleagues is limited. The method they use to get their message across may be as important as the content itself.

It may help to establish some guidelines for effective communication. The following list is based on the principles in Joan Dean's book *Managing the Primary School:*

— Teachers are more likely to be responsive to the advice of coordinators if addressed personally rather than anonymously in a staff meeting or by memo.

— Coordinators need to learn that with teachers, just as with children, rousing the listener's interest is necessary, in order to get your message across.

— Information is more likely to be valued if it gives an advantage in power or status to the listener.

— No-one likes to let down their team or working group. It is sometimes desirable therefore for coordinators to present their information in a way that requires action.

— Teachers, changed with the responsibility of promoting curricular areas to their colleagues, may find an advantage in choosing an appropriate messenger. The status of the source of information is often seen to indicate its importance.

— The situation (surroundings, time of day etc.) should be chosen carefully in order to predispose the listener to be receptive.

Making Meetings Effective

Meetings are the most common method that coordinators use to get their message over, but they are not always a success. Just having a meeting is not enough. The prime consideration must be 'What do you want to happen at the meeting?' This point is seldom addressed. You may wish to call a meeting to:

Communicate information

Subject coordinators will often need to give information to their colleagues, such as the dates and location of a local history and geography book exhibition, the list of computer programs bought by the PTA, and so on. Often this information can be given out in written form with only a brief explanation and possibly without having a meeting at all. The skill is to ensure that the information is read and acted upon. Wasting everyone's time for an hour, to compensate for your lack of foresight in not preparing a briefing sheet, does not go down well with busy teachers.

Generate discussion

If you want teachers to discuss issues, they need to be properly prepared beforehand by being given the relevant information. You may need to arrange the seating in a way that everyone can see each other in order to encourage participation. A brainstorming session recorded on tape can generate ideas or possible solutions.

The key to success for this type of meeting is to create an atmosphere which encourage staff to share ideas and perceptions. They will not do this if early statements are not accepted, at least as starting points, for the generation of further ideas.

Make corporate decisions

If coordinators are organising a meeting to reach a key decision on a key topic, it is vital that everyone is aware of the meeting's purpose. Time has to be allowed beforehand, so that small group meetings can already have aired some issues. Make sure teachers have had time to read and absorb printed material. Decide before the meeting if you intend to take a vote (if necessary) or whether it would be more appropriate to continue the debate until a consensus is reached.

Coordinators will be more effective if they understand the difference between the various purposes of these staff meetings and realise what can go wrong. We have all attended meetings which were monopolised by one person, had too many important items left to the end, or failed to get people involved. Occasionally all these things happen in one meeting. We have also all attended well run friendly and relaxed meetings which kept to the point and were time will spent.

Coordinators need to consider a variety of strategies for organising and chairing meetings. Their aim should be to ensure that as many as possible of the negative features are avoided and the positive ones achieved. In *The Primary School Management Book* written by David Playfoot, Martin Skelton and Geoff Southworth further useful information can be found on the conduct of effective meetings in schools.

Meetings also have another purpose in the primary school. By passing the chairmanship around, headteachers can demonstrate a commitment to and support for those appointed to coordination posts. This will allow coordinators to practise skills which they will need as they develop in their careers.

BIBLIOGRAPHY

Belbin, R.M. *Management Teams: Why they Succeed or Fail,* Heinemann, Oxford, 1981.

2
LEARNING EXPERIENCES OF 13-YEAR-OLDS

During a severe afternoon thunderstorm on a late April week end, Richard had a close call with a lightning bolt. He and his fellow boy scouts were camping in a tall timber stand in the mountains. During the height of the storm, when all were huddled in their pup tents, lightning struck a pine tree in the centre of their camp. It was the very tree to which Richard had tied the guy rope supporting the rear pole of his tent. Some of the electricity leaped along the wet rope and decended the rear tent pole with a shower of sparks. This together with the tremendous thunderclap which followed, made a lasting impression on Richard and his buddy, Jim even though neither was hurt. When the boys returned to school on the following Monday, a lively discussion broke forth in Mr. Kenneth Torgerson's science class.[1] Richard had asked, "What causes lightning?" Learning begins with such a question. The learning process in school or in the boy scout camp should be a quest, essentially a pursuit of problems significant to the children here and now, and a progressive development of insight into the nature of man and of the universe.

Teachers often think in terms of ultimate goals and objectives in a course of study. Children think mainly in terms of answers to their questions, asked or unasked. Richard wanted an answer to his question about lightning and its genesis in a thundercloud. Richard was thinking in terms of a specific answer. He had not yet set up goals or objectives beyond and encompassing that specific answer. Whether he would depended chiefly upon Mr. Torgerson or perhaps one of the participants in the discussion. Mr. Torgerson suggested that the group might have to learn about several other factors in a thunderstorm before lightning could be understood. As a teacher, he was aware that the question could not be given adequate treatment until the problem area had been expanded to include an inquiry into the mysteries of the thunderstorm as a whole. Lightning is only a part of the whole phenomenon. It cannot be understood as a part. Understanding lightning awaits an inquiry into the role which it plays in the total weather pattern. Thus, Mr. Torgerson sought to lead the pupils toward investigation of all of the dynamics of a thunderstorm. Should they, he knew that the perception of Richard and of the other eventually would expand to include a rather complex group of weather factors, and, further, that an understanding or insight relative to lightning would come only after these factors had been brought into focus for the students.

A CLASS PROJECT ON WEATHER

Mr. Torgerson could have shut off the learning process quickly by giving Richard a one-sentence definition of lightning and asking him to remember the words. Mr. Torgerson knew, however, the value of pursuit in learning. Here was an interest in lightning that could lead to many significant learnings in his class. He knew, moreover, the value of working with the tide of the learner's motivation. Richard was not always conscious of achieving goals which Mr. Torgerson may have set for him. He really did not pause long enough to consider. To have done so would have thrown him off the track. He was exploring questions *be* had asked and he wanted to know the answers.

Richard's learning, which began with the bolt of lightning, continued at home and at school. By raising the question in his class on Monday morning, he stimulated considerable interest among his classmates, especially as he hold of his vivid experience with lightning in the mountains. He interlarded his discussion with several rhetorical questions which began with, "Did you know that —?" His new but, as yet, untested learnings gained on the mountain were thus shared with the group. This led to additional sharing of information in the group and, subsequently, to more unanswered questions. These promoted a class project on weather.

The Committee on Thunderstorms

Richard's original question about lightning had now influenced directly the school curriculum. His interest and his study had been contagious. A whole class went off in hot pursuit. Richard became chairman of a committee on thunderstorms.

Mr. Torgerson continued to direct the discussion in Richard's committee by asking such questions as, "If one has to look into a whole storm to discover the secret of lightning from a thundercloud, what other forces might we find in the cloud? Do these relate to the ground or other clouds?"

Jim volunteered that there is water vapor or droplets in the clouds. Stephen said that there is wind in the cloud. Mark said hail, sometimes. George observed that dust particles must be in the cloud, taken there by the terrific up-drafts of warms air from the ground.

Mr. Torgerson broke in to point out that the winds in the cloud might need to be studied further. He asked, "If there is hot air in the cloud might there also be cold air?" Richard replied, "There must be cold air in the cloud because the wind which came with the rain in the afternoon was colder than the wind we had near noon." "Yes," said Jim. "This cold air must have come from the cloud; where else could it have come from?" Mr. Torgerson interjected. "George had suggested that there are up-drafts of warm air in the cloud. I suppose that most of you have leaned from your previous science studies that warm air tends to rise, that it expands when heated and becomes lighter. What happens to air when it is cooled?" "It condenses, gets heavier, and settles toward the earth," replied George. "That proves it!" Exclaimed Jim who was quick to see the relation between his theory about how the cold air arrived at their camp and George's generalization. "This cold air came down out of the cloud."

Mr. Torgerson pursued this line of reasoning , "If cold air and hot air come in contact with each other, what happens? " The students were quick to respond with their own versions of how the air currents in the thundercloud were characterized by up-drafts and down-drafts. They were quick to sense that cold air masses and warm air masses under certain condition could product tornadoes. After considerable discussion of air currents, Mr. Torgerson led the discussion to a consideration of how these air currents were related to rain, hail snow, and lightning. The problem, having been expanded earlier to include the system or whole within which lightning was a part, now was becoming differentiated as the problem-solving process reached detailled analysis. Eventually, Richard achieved an insight into the "why" of lightning when the various factors operating to produce it came into focus for him. This insight was but one of many which Richard gained from his quest. Some of these insights led to further questions and therefore to other voyages of discovery.

Neither living nor learning can be switched off or on conveniently like the mechanical brain. Neither can be transferred to yesterday or pushed forward to tomorrow. Richard's question about lightning could not wait. Living and learning simply take place in the active present. Richard had had a vivid experience but lacked insights with which to interpret that experience.

Whether experiences were direct or vicarious, he profited from them because of his needs and purposes. He eagerly used books on weather, weather maps, drawings of clouds and air currents, various instruments for measuring and reading air pressure and humidity. He made many materials and instruments for his own use or to show others what he had learned. He discussed and listened. He read and observed. He imagined thought, recreated drew together, and gereralized. He did all of these things and more, not because someone force him, but because the force was inner and personal.

He learned much from books from interview from maps, from the discussions of his classmates, etc., and he learned effectively from these various second-hand sources because he had had sufficient first-hand experiences to make the vicarious ones meaningful. The fact that fundamental learning which involves new generalization or insights is after critically related to direct concrete experience was particularly true of Richard's learning.

The Committee on Causes of Weather[2]

The committee on causes of weather decided to review basic date about seasonal changes before going deeply into the causes of weather. Mary Jane had been asked to review this information and present it to the committee.

"First, I would like to show you why winter is cold and summer is hot. I will use the globe and this lamp, " began Mary Jane. "While our planet spins around on its own axis, it also circles the sun. Every round trip takes a year. Since the earth's axis is tilted, first one hemisphere and then the other leans toward the sun. See now when our northern half of the earth is tilted toward the sun, we have summer. " Now Mary Jane walked around to the other side of the desk. "Oh," commented Matched, "when the northern half of the earth leans away from the sun our days are short." "That's right," agreed Mary Jane. "Anyone can walk around the light now and see for himself."

"That was very nice, Mary Jane, " Mr. Torgerson congratulated her. "Let me ask you about this. Can you think of any other reason why the summer days are so much hotter than winter days besides the fact that they are longer?

" I know," said John. "In book I was reading this morning it showed that in summer the sunlight was more direct, like a straight line, while in the winter it was slanted."

"Oh, I can see that! " said Mary Jane.

"Would you show the others with the globe and the light?" Mr. Torgerson suggested. Mary Jane agreed, "All right. See how the light is shining brightly on that part of the globe that is tilted toward the sun? The lower part is almost in shadow."

Mr. Torgerson moved on the another subgroup talking about an experiment.

"How are you coming along? Let's see, you decided you would show us about clouds."

"Oh, yes," said John, "I wanted to ask you something. Is it all right if we do this experiment to show the class what a cloud is?

Mr. Torgerson read the page in the book which John had spread out in front of him. "That really does explain cloud formation clearly, John. Why don't you go down to the cafeteria and get a milk bottle and put some water in it like the book says and we'll try it first to see if it works."

While the committee was waiting for John to return, Mr. Torgerson got a box of matches out of his desk drawer. Presently, John came in with the bottle. "Now you read the directions to us, Cathy, please," John said, as she stood holding the bottle.

Cathy started, "Wet the inside of a clean milk bottle with warm water."

"Yes, we already did that. Go on," urged Johnny.

"Drop a lighted match into the bottle."

"Oh," said Johnny, "where will we get the match?"

"Here, John, I have some," Mr. Torgerson said, giving him the box. He opened it and took one out. Jemmy reminded Johnny of previously learned safety rules. "Don't forget to close the box, John, " he said . " Oh, that's right," John said as he closed the box. He lit the match and dropped it into the bottle.

"Why, it went out," Cathy said.

"Sure, don't you remember there isn't enough air in it to burn, or for combustion, " John replied.

"Why did we put the match in? What does that have to do with making the cloud?" protested Jimmy

"It says here in the book," said Cathy, " that the match goes out immediately, but leaves a dense trail of smoke. The smoke supplies specks around which the moisture can condense."

"Oh, yew, I can see the smoke," said Johnny.

"Now," Cathy continued reading, "stand with your back toward the lights so you can see what happens. Suck the air out of the bottle and a cloud forms inside."

"Yes, it does," said Johnny, "See!"

"I wonder why that is, " said Cathy.

"Well, students," said Mr. Torgerson, "It looks as if you have a lot of reading and information to get if you re to be able to answer the class's questions. You can start with the science books on the side table and if you need any more, I will be glad to help you a little more later on," he said, as he moved on to the next committee.

The Committee on Weather Forecasting

The committee which was to find out about weather forecasting wanted unanimously to have Mr. Paul Plunkett, a local television weather forecaster, visit the class and give a talk on how to forecast weather.

After further committee discussion, it was agreed that they should write a letter to Mr. Plunkett inviting him to give a talk to the class. Mary Kay then asked how this letter should be worded, and it was apparent to the committee that they needed a review of letter writing skills, Mr. Torgerson launched the committee upon the study of letter construction. Each child wrote one or two drafts, with the teacher making the proper corrections until a suitable one was selected to be mailed.

Larry then asked what questions they should ask Mr. Plunkett. Each pupil was to write down what he or she considered to be good questions—pertinent to what the committee was working on. Here are two samples of questions listed. Where so you obtain your weather information? Are weather reports reliable? Before Mr. Plunkett's visit, Mr. Torgerson suggested that this might be a good time to review the rules for good listeners as well as those for common courtesy.

During Paul Plunkett's visit the children asked him whether he had any written materials which he could make available to the class. He presented the class with a number of pamphlets. These provided another source of information for the committees. Also the children asked him to comment on the daily weather chart which they had started. He offered them some suggestions on making the symbols, and complemented them on their neat work.

The committee voted to have Bruce call and thank Mr. Plunkett for his most interesting talk and suggestions.

When the children found out from Paul Plunkett that he relied on the Weather Bureau for much of his information, Larry wondered if his committee could visit the weather station at the airport to send how they gather their information. In talking to Mr. Plunkett, they realized that they might be able to do some forecasting themselves, and Alice suggested that they could find out how to read a weather map. Alice had clipped the weather report from the morning paper. Jack wondered how the Weather Bureau received the information form other cities. Fay said that when they lived in Washington, D.C., she could dial a telephone number and get a recorded weather forecast. Larry volunteered to call the Weather Bureau to see if he could arrange a visit. This was an opportunity to discuss telephone manners, how to introduce oneself, and to briefly and clearly state one's business. The committee then discussed what they wanted to learn at the Weather Bureau if the trip could be arranged.

At this point, Mr. Torgerson suggested that this might be a worthwhile trip for the whole class, and the committee invited the other committees to share this experience with them. All committees consulted their lists of question to see which ones could be answered at the Weather Bureau. They decided upon the questions to ask and suggested that each take a notebook and pencil for note taking. Alice said that her father who is and aviator told her that the weather map is printed as it comes over a sort of teletype machine and she wanted to see that. Them they arrived at their destination, the and girls were given and opportunity to look about and to ask questions. The purpose of the trip was constantly kept in mind and the children's attention focused on the things that would answer their questions. They found but what the weather symbols on the chart mean and decided that they could use the same symbols on their own map. They learned how to read barometer and found out why a barometer is important in forecasting. In fact, they were surprised to find out that they could make simplified versions of most of these instruments.

They watched a weather balloon being sent aloft and heard how it radioed information. Later they secured one of these balloons for their own classroom, the better to analyze its operations.

By the time their visit was over, the children had learned how weather is forecast, and they could reproduce many of the activities of the weather station in their own class room.

The children were sufficiently well prepared for the trip so as to ensure desirable behaviour. Each child had certain questions he wanted answered, and he was responsible for taking notes so that he could share what he had learned.

In following up the trip in the next committee meeting, the children were given and opportunity to freely express their reactions and comments. Then the original questions were checked to determine how many could be answered from the new information learned on the trip. A chart was made to record the most important learnings gained from the trip in order to emphasize the most valuable ideas. The information gathered was then used in planning what activities the children could carry out in their classroom and at home.

They had learned how to read a weather map and had added to their vocabularies such words as meteorologist, Fahrenheit, occluded front, cold front, warm front stationary front, isobars, high and low pressure areas, and anemometer. Alice volunteered to clip the weather map out of the morning paper and bring it to school every day. But they all agreed that daily weather maps are not up-to-the-minute and that they cover general conditions for large areas of the country. So they concluded they really needed their own weather station. The aerologist had given them some ideas of things they could make and their reference material had lots of different suggestion. So they made a list of the different kinds of information that would be most useful, and how they could get that information from equipment they could build. The list included: wet and dry bulb hygrometer, rain gauge, anemometer, wind vane, barometer, cloud direction indicator, and air movement indicator. These could all be made from simple materials available at home, in school, and in the corner drugstore.

The committee spent the next two or three days assembling and constructing the instruments for their weather station. When each was completed the person who made it set up a chart or a notebook for daily weather observations, which he transferred to a large weather chart. When their daily observations were complete, the committee as a group verified and interpreted their data and arrived at their daily weather forecast, which they took turns posting on the bulletin board each day.

When their forecast proved to be wrong, they inquired into the reason why. In this way they learned from their own experience why professional forecasters are not always accurate.

The Committee on Weather Records

In the group working on weather instruments there had been the problem of "Just how shall we present our findings to the class?" Sue suggested a list of the temperatures for the past three weeks which she had been recording. Bill, who was interested in arithmetic, mentioned that he had seen some pictures with bars on them and others with lines which showed the number of sales made by salesmen with whom his father works. Could this be used to show the different temperatures?" he asked. Here the teacher stepped in to capitalize on the opportunity to teach bar and line graphs. Some suggestions were made to look in the arithmetic book to see if the group could find out if and how Bill's idea might really work. The necessity for neatness and accuracy were emphasized. The teacher them suggested to Bill that he should try to learn as much as he could about the construction of graphs and how to interpret them so that he would be able to explain the charts to the class.

Getting back to Bob's interest in new words, the teacher asked him to see if there were any other new words in the arithmetic book in the material on graphs that might be useful also. Bob searched the arithmetic book for new words, and by reading it also learned about graphs; but he had been activated by a different appeal than Bill, who would have studied about grapes just because they were in his favourite textbook.

But what about Betty? Her favorite activity was art work. How was she encouraged to study graphs? The teacher suggested she look in the text to see how the graphs were made and encouraged her to try to make her graphs of temperatures as attractive as possible by using good colour combinations and appropriate captions. Several days later Betty came up with this idea: " I saw several line graphs with more than one line on each. Couldn't we take the temperature several times a day—say, in the morning before school, at noon, and after school and show this on a line graph with three different colored lines?" The teacher overheard this and interrupted: " I think your idea is good, so why don't you make a graph with the three lines and we'll post it on the main bulletin board for our school. Them we will all be able to check the temperatures every day." the private thought behind this is , "Good. Now I've found a way to keep them interested in continuing their learning about wheather even after we start on something new in class. It will also help cement their understanding about graphs." Doubtless, Betty's artistic graphs would arouse equations from the other students in other rooms also.

The committee also decided to draws a large map of the United States. Johnny said. " Then we can print the names of various states and cities on it, and cach day we will put tags on the board showing high and low temperatures at each city." " Yes," Anne added, "we will also show with different colored pencils where it is snowing and raining. We can do this by checking the weather map clipped from the morning paper." Through this project the children could see how temperatures vary United States. Jim volunteered to keep a chart of the high and low temperatures at fifteen different cities so they could be compared with local temperatures. From this the class also could figure out the mean daily temperature in various cities.

They decided to follow the course of the weather across the United States: warm fronts, cold fronts, high and low pressure areas. Eventually, the map became a permanent display in the classroom to be referred to again and again, a source of pride for the original committee members.

Study and Reporting Skills

Out of this search for answers came certain teaching opportunities. This project afforded an opportunity for the teacher to develop in the pupils a further understanding of how libraries can be used as a source of information in problem-solving. The teacher explained the weather project to the librarian and she supplemented the work of the teacher by helping the children in the use of the library facilities. The teacher prepared his class for utilization of the materials in the library by first teaching them to use the table of contents, index, alphabet and simple reference materials in the room. The group discussion reiterated the proper attitudes and behaviour of people using a library and the reasons for these. On the first visit, the teacher accompanied the whole class while the librarian, who knew the children's needs in advance, explained to them the use of the card catalog, the encyclopedia, atlases, charts, dictionaries, and almanacs, and assisted them in locating the books they needed. After this introduction, the students were allowed to go to the library individually or as committee to work by themselves whenever possible. They learned to find their way in a library first by locating simple materials and then as they gained confidence, by searching for more conclusive inching material. In the library situation the work of the teacher and the librarian was a cooperative endeavor, and the results were most satisfying when the group reached the point where the students were able to find independently the information then needed and were able to distinguish between reliable and unreliable sources of information.

When periodicals were available, the students were encouraged to use them. Mr. Torgerson provided mimeographed lists giving the names and issues of periodicals and the titles of books useful as source material. Johnny is an above average student and came to Mr. Torgerson for suggestions for outside reading in connection with his committee work. Mr. Torgerson guided him in the use of the *Reader's Guide to Periodical Literature* and encouraged him to share with the others those things which he found to be of particular interest and which provided further insight into the answers for the common question. In this sharing experience Johnny made use of his reading skills—scanning, outlining, etc.—and of his writing and speaking skills. Though the entire class had had prior instruction in these skills, Mr. Torgerson decided to bring the whole class together again for further work on these skills.

Each Friday all committees reported on the week's activities to the entire class. This gave the class the opportunity to reevaluate its plans and goals. This was a learning opportunity for the whole class, not only in the use of communication skills but also to promote skills in organizing material and in critical thinking. Each student was encouraged to relate his committee's work to the contribution of each committee member and all other committees and to determine values in reference to the common goals. This self-evaluatioin procedure may well be one of the most important skills that the students learn throughout their entire school experience therefore it should never be neglected by the teacher.

The students were proud of the results of their work and together decided to invite other eighth graders to share in their learning experiences. Considerable art work had been done, from the making of scrapbooks by individuals on such subjects as "Unusual Weather Phenomena" to a whole committee executing a mural on cloud formations. These and the many permanent weather instruments and the charts and graphs were proudly displayed. The students planned a simulated television program to entertain their guests.

SUMMARY

From Richard's specific experience with lightning, his learning grew in several directions. His study of air movements in thunderclouds led to a study of air movements in particular types of clouds, and from there to a study of air movements in polar fronts and warm fronts. A study of air currents in the cloud led to an understanding that a gigantic amount of static electricity is generated by these air currents as then create friction with millions of dust particles and water droplets in the cloud; this to study of other ways kin which electricity is generated. He broadened his knowledge of the water cycle, heat radiation, air pressure and other properties of the atmosphere. Many other questions arose in the pursuit of the original problem; many other answers had to be found including how storms affect air travel.

In the pursuit of such self-selected problems, moreover, he and his fellow student acquire new skills in arithmetic reading, spelling, writing, and composition. For many pupils in the class there were great strides in skill development in response to and obvious need in the tasks selected. They learned many new concepts in history, physics, geography, and a host of subject fields. These concepts and skills were eagerly learned by the pupils when they saw that such learnings were essential to completion of tasks which they had selected.

REFERENCES

1. Doolen Junior High School, Tucson, Ariz.
2. The author is indebted to student teachers Arthur Munoz, Margaret Trachta, Margaret Read, Don Schoan, Phillip Alsworth, and Helen Dick for help in recording the experiences of the three committees on causes of weather, weather forecasting and weather records.

3

CURRICULUM CHANGE AS AN ASPECT OF CULTURAL CHANGE

THE NEED FOR CURRICULUM CHANGE

America may look back upon a half-century of tentative changes, experimentation, reaction, and retrenchment in its far-flung system of public education. In contrast, tremendous and irreversible changes have taken place in the culture during the same period. These changes in the culture are not merely continuing; they are accelerating. By very nature, these cultural changes are marking education more a problem every day. Thus, education has become one of the chief manifestations of cultural lag in this century. In no area of human endeavour is there greater danger of cultivating superficial and conventional habits than in teaching. Culturally speaking, this *crystalization* is common historically, exemplified in any practice or institution that has become fixed and habitual and remains so in the face of change beyond its usefulness, and thus exhibits cultural lag. Crystallization in changing world like that of the twentieth century can be costly and even disastrous. Today's educational system undoubtedly is characterized by much crytallization, and since education has become so important to the survival of mankind and its institutions, this cultural lag represents peril.

THE INTERACTION OF THE CURRICULUM AND THE CULTURAL

Ideally, education is immediately interactive with the culture. It cannot be unaffected by the continuous process of change going on in the culture. The role of education in the culture is not restricted to initiate the young into the mores of the older social group. It participates in the broader process of cultural rebirth — rebirth frequently marked by mutation.[1] To the extent that education touches every age group, all members of the society may be participating simultaneously in this process of rebirth. Cultural rebirth and mutation take place whenever there is learning, problem-solving, reconstruction of experience, socialization, and creativity. All of these are characteristic of the democratic problem solving curriculum. In such a curriculum design, the prime, interactive relationship of curriculum change and cultural change are built in.

In an era of tremendous cultural change, the interactive relationship of cultural and the curriculum unfortunately has not been achieved successfully in all areas. Apparently, America has never developed a truly American curriculum in harmony with the other dynamic aspects of life in the New World. It has been a slave of tradition and pseudo values in an era when the culture and the society have been achieving history's most dynamic growth. In 1926, Harold Rugg made the dramatic statement that: "Not once in a century and a half of national history has the curriculum of the school caught up with the dynamic content of American life."[2]

Rapid, accelerating bewildering, uncontrolled change is even more characteristics of today than of 1926. With the rapid expansion of the school to admit all the children of all the people, education was pictured in 1938 as lacking the courage of decision by Lloyd Cook, who added: "It is said to lack direction and effectiveness .... Education, once so patently the solution for all of our social problems, has itself become a major problem."[3] The schools appeared, further, to have lost their way in the strange new world of technological progress, swelling population, fast communication, urban-suburban trends, heterogeneous ethnic groups, and extremes of individual mobility.

In 1946, Alice Miel observed that in spite of tremendous efforts towards curriculum improvement during the previous two decades, it was rather generally agreed that very little fundamental change had taken place in the curriculum during a time of rapid and drastic change in the cultural field surrounding the school.[4] More than a decade later, the curriculum of the typical American school does not now reflect, nor is it making much process toward catching up with, the dynamic forces of our national life.

THE CHALLENGE FOR AMERICAN EDUCATION

Chief among the challenges for American education are demands for a greater emphasis on the development of a new generation (1) far moire psychologically mature than the present one, (2) with democracy entrenched in its value system and its behaviour, (3) knowledge and understanding more than its predecessors, and (4) equipped with the attitudes and skills of the scientific method in order that it may meet the unknown and even unimaginable problems of its tomorrow.

Although some progress has been made in a few schools toward the development of curricula which can help pupils achieve these ends, harsh realities must force educators and the public to the conclusion that the typical school curricuium has changed little, perhaps because of faulty insight, neglected opportunities, or fear of public reprisal. Numerous sincere attempts at curriculum development programs in recent years which yielded only paper changes present a rather sad picture. The regular failure of such course of study rewriting or memo-writing projects to produce anything other than superficial results has doomed this type of program to a deserved oblivion.

Course-of-study rewriting and other paper changes have little significance in the task ahead. The changes must be made in people, in their personalities and in their ways of doing things.

Change in the personalities of professional school personnel should include new insights into the significance of curriculum process, new attitudes towards learners and the role of the teacher, and a higher level of personal maturity. Attitudes toward doing, however, are even more significant. It is important that teachers and administrators demonstrate their willingness to experiment with process, to change their ways of doing things on the job. In this case, experiencing is the only effective teacher. Cooperative effort and team-play will offer security, critical analysis, and evaluation.

Thus, the teacher profession has had thrust upon it a tremendous responsibility. Even though it has not always been backed, or even usually, by a large segment of the public in its attempts to establish a curriculum consistent with educational research and the changing culture, the profession has no choice but to face up to the present challenge. Far too much is at stake, both for the profession and for the future of America.

Concepts presented in the following pages of this chapter should be carefully evaluated by professional personnel at all levels for their value in orienting the whole profession towards the task which lies before it. The concepts of (1) culture and its dynamic components, (2) how cultural change takes place (3) how this basic process is related to curriculum change, and (4) how the American social crisis and its educational crisis are different aspects of the same condition—all are analyzed for those responsible for curriculum development.

THE NATURE OF CULTURAL CHANGE

Culture and its Components

Culture is everything created by the hand or by the mind of man. It is both the material and nonmaterial. It is the ways of behaving and ways of thinking. It is product. It is the machine that makes them. It is technological data that give rise to the machine. It is human thought that develops the technology. It is the value system which determines how man shall use his creation. It is the totality of everything man-made.

White the natural environment may contribute to cultural change, it is outside structure of culture; its effect on change is governed by the principle by which any outside factor affects change. The most useful division of culture into components appears in that of Sorokin:

1. The *ideological* component—all meanings, value, tested thought, mores, and norms.
2. The *behavioral* component—all actions, reactions, interactions or behaviour of the human agents.
3. The *material* component—all machines, all nonhuman vehicles, materials, energies and concrete tools.[5]

These are integral components of the whole and are insignificant as mere parts because of their relative and dynamic interaction with the whole. This is an organic concept of culture which assigns no meaning to any of the components in isolation. Components, therefore, take on meaning only in relation to the other components and to the whole culture.

Society is the behavioral component, the human agents and their interactions. Human behaviour can be observed only in present relationships which cannot stand still, and that behaviour is so bound up causally with the other components of culture, the terms *society* and *social change* cannot be wrenched out of the behavioral component, or *field,* even for purposes of study. If society is to be changed or directed, the social architect may select any component of the culture of precipitate change. Since the components are interrelated causally, a change in one will mean ultimately a change in all. Thus, society does not operate without a value system and a material culture. Social change, then, is an aspect of a larger cultural change. If the eductor wants to change people in order, to change the curriculum, he must understand the *field* or component nature of cultural change.

When one of the components of culture undergoes change, whether precipitated from within or from without, there may be a lapse of time before corresponding changes take place in the other components. If so, a cultural lag appears. This lag creates a maladjustment in the whole—a disequilibrium or tension—which demands resolution according to the law of *closure.* When the social scientist or educator can determine which of the components is involved in the lag, efforts should be concentrated upon that particular component to remove the disharmonious elements which apparently are preventing change. The relationship among components will be dynamic unless crytallization has taken place within one or more of them which prevents a nature interaction. *Crystallization* is the formation of a set pattern or habitual response arising from the cultural lag which no longer yields to creativity or new thought.

What does the term *dynamics* mean? Dynamics refers to the relative forces or factors in a system, as, for example, the components of the culture. In a dynamic theory such forces never reach a perfect equilibrium; thus, change tends to be constant and continuous. Change may be controlled, slowed, accelerated, or channeled by manipulating its dynamics but never stopped. Inevitably any social system changes as long as it continues to function.

The possibility of channeling change lies in utilizing a precipitant situation, that is, a perceived need or problem as the entering wedge. Social change apparently is most likely to take place when tensions arise in the culture. Thinking undoubtedly is indispensable to this process. Indeed, social change is not unlike learning. In modern

American society, the tensions are many and deep because of the conflicting interests of groups who want to control the tremendous technological or material culture. Under an uncertain national ideology, the conflicting parties tend to use belligerence rather than mutual deliberation. Communication breaks down and understanding is underdeveloped. The situation presented in not unlike an unorganized group of children whose home values differ greatly and who, lacking a common goal or set of standards which could be developed under the guidance of the school, resort to a jungle behaviour. The strong of the moment win out over the weak. Prejudice is substituted for empathy. Materials become concentrated in the hands of a few. Group solidarity breaks down. Real suffering comes to some. Relief can come only when the group, usually as a result of some outside stimulus, adopts a common aim and sets up machinery for deliberation and evaluation, for division of labor and sharing. Again, the role of a common ideology and an organization of behaviours in relation to it is the critical requirement. The teacher, the curriculum specialist, the statement, all share in this knowledge of how social change must be motivated.

The development or growing process of culture is effected by the continuous creative interaction of internal as well as external forces when precise methods for resolving differences in society have been set up. The appeal to reason is not automatic. It requires a framework by methodology as well as a set of principles. When present, these make the whole process of social change as simple as learning.

The culture, so organized, will act constantly to preserve its unity by conditioning its internal parts and by resisting external factors which threaten this unity. The whole maintains its unity even throughout the process of adding and discarding nonessential or nonpatterned elements. Any change in a major component, however, changes the whole. Thus, while the precipitant which upsets equilibrium may come from inside or outside the culture, only a change in the value system would result in the culture's facing in a new direction.

Any institution of the culture has the three major components, either one of which can be marked for change by selecting the appropriate precipitant. The community, the family, the school, the church, the corporation, the government, or any other system, all have ideological behavioral, and material components. A change either in the material setting or tools, in the human agents or their ways of interacting, or in the creed, the knowledge, or the way of thinking will produce modification in the quality and the function of the whole system.

Technology and Cultural Change

Ogburn[6] maintains that the material culture tends to grow faster than the nonmaterial. This creates a lag in the nonmaterial culture. This lag of the social aspects of culture appears to be the usual aftermath of mechanical invention or discover. Some mechanical inventions may effect immediate social changes and the combined effect of the two may cause a rupture in the culture as a whole.

The new elements of culture are added by invention, discovery, and diffusion. If an element is not invented or discovered within a culture, it may be borrowed from without. Diffusion refers to this borrowing process. All culture are great borrowers. The nonmaterial culture is not borrowed so readily as the material, and when the former is borrowed, it usually undergoes substantial modification before fitting into the new culture pattern. Every invention is the result of an evolutionary process. Very few inventions are lost because of the bequeathment of the heritage from one generation to another, education, written records, and tangible products. Therefore culture accumulates, too. Inventions tend to increase very much as the number of ancestors increase for each succeeding generation. As the base of accumulating inventions grows large, more and better inventions are made probable. This causes an acceleration cultural change. For these reasons, Ogburn saw no limit to the speed of change in the future barring a catastrophe of gigantic proportions which would destroy a great body of the accumulated inventions of mankind.[7]

Change in technology cause variations in institutions and customs. Women began to drive automobiles is great numbers after the invention of the self-starter. This change cause changes in the habits of women regarding mobility, home life, care of children, vacationing and use of hotels. Important inventions are seldom limited to a single-social effect. Ogburn maintains that the effects of an invention like the radio are multiple and spread out like the spokes of a wheel. He lists no less than one hundred and fifty such social effect from the invention of the radio.[8]

The Primary of Society or Technology?

While Ogburn would explain social change primarily by the

advancing technology culture, MacIver would consider society or human interaction as primary. The social process given rise to products, machines, and technology. The structure of society consists of present relationship whose equilibrium is constantly changing. Cultural change emerges from social change and enters the history of civilization at a later time.[9] Further, social structures or relationship are not like artifacts which may be placed in a museum to be observed and saved from deterioration. Social phenomena are historical in the sense that they continue. Society is a becoming. It is a process and not a product.

Even if human nature did not change, the conditions under which it expresses itself are constantly changing. The environment of man changes, partly because of forces with which he can do little or nothing, and partly because of the designs of men. Every change in the relationship of man to his environment means in turn some change in his relationship to the follow. Instability and change are, therefore, inherent in human society. Since nothing is independent of the universe about it, the process involves interaction and adaptation with the larger environment. Thus, the process of social evolution is a dynamic continuous interaction of all factors of human existence. It is sharply distinguished from the concept of progress. It may have its ups and its downs, its backward as well as its forward movements in terms of social scale, but all this is considered quite irrelevant. Rise and decay of systems is to be explained by man's dynamic assessments and the conjuncture of social forces. The group, by its choices of alternatives within the total matrix of forces and factors, determines its own rise or decay.[10]

The Field Nature of Cultural Change

The confusion of the role of technology in cultural evolution is cleared, thinks Sorokin,[11] by realizing that it is the body of testes thought in science and not machines themselves which really explains technical progress. A backward nation may import machines from this country but be longsuffering in its attempt to use them until the know-how also is imported or developed. The technological inventions are only vehicles. Most cultural relationships are configurative with meaningful, casual relationships with other parts of the cultural. Yet, it must be recognized, thinks Sorokin, that some relationship are chance relationships between nonpatterned factors. These latter make for the sometimes gross and imperfect configurations of social phenomena. True meaningful-causal relationship are more typical, however, and furnish the basis for most organization in social situations. Man can gain control of these situations by understanding and shaping the meanings, the behaviours, and the materials which structure them.[12]

No idea can stand still. It is subject to change as it is pondered over by human beings. Values contain in themselves many implications and, sometimes, hidden contradictions. These many possibilities and potentialities cannot be fully grasped at any given time, but become explicit as the process of human contemplation unfolds.[13] The more universal or general the idea, the deeper are its hidden implications. Some systems of meanings do not become objectified fully, lacking proper human or material vehicles. Failures may occur due to immaturity of the concept, the lack of sufficient technical skill, the lack of prime existence of all its components, or the hostility of other systems.[14]

Any on-going system changes inevitably as long as it continues to function. Functioning cultural systems have this inherent property of change. The probability of their change is increased by the social milieu which consists of many changing systems. This total configuration of interacting system will of necessity intensify the change of member systems. Each member system, changing and accumulating consequences of each change, continuously transforms both itself and its milieu. The unique character of the system is not sacrificed through interaction with other systems; this unique character constantly unfolds its inherent potentialities. The external factors of interaction act mainly to accelerate or retard the change of a system and to modify its secondary characteristics. External factors do not transform a system into something basically different from its inherent nature.[15]

Societies are integrated and mature in correspondence with the operation of a rule which permits its members to live together and work together in relative peace and harmony. Sorokin claims that the reason for peace between nations, if such exists, is the operation of the golden rule between them. The disintegration of values relative to the golden rule within a society gives rise to civil strife or even civil war, and among nations leads to world war.[16]

IMPLICATIONS OF CULTURAL DYNAMICS FOR CURRICULUM CHANGE

Implications for Ideological Change

The existence of great ideals and cultural goal in American literature, history, and art cannot be denied. The chasm between these traditional ideals of the nation and the actual beliefs and behaviours of the people in the present seriously weakens the influence of this country as a leader in international affairs and prevents progress toward a more mature society. The American social system is characterized by great strain between its ideological and its behavioural components. There is a vast difference between what may American *profess* and what they *do.* They often profess to believe one way but act in another. They "talk" democracy but do not behave democratically either at home or abroad. They decry communist materialism but the people of the world seem to remember best America's own materialism. Christian ethics are give much lip service in this country but seldom do they govern observed action. Everywhere *behavior has mocked stated ideals.*

Emphasis in this country has been placed on the professed or stated ideology of the people. Perhaps many people of the present generation are ignorant of the behavioral process which could carry their started ideals into action. However, it is more likely that a frightening number of Americans do not actually believe in their professed ideals. It is probable that they do not fail to behave appropriately in terms of their *actual* ideals—ideals that no one would dare to profess publicly. The drive toward correct public behavior has led many to compartmentalized thinking. Too often, ethical or religious beliefs have no place in the conduct of business and apparently, "All's fair in love and politics," is an actual and private belief of many.

How much responsibility must American education share for this state of affairs? The potentially great ideology of America apparently has never been consolidated nor taught effectively in its schools. It is no wonder that our soldiers sometimes declare "We don't know what we are fighting for." In harrowing battle field circumstances, the traditional national slogans sound hollow to them. They never achieved real faith or conviction in these remote ideals. Many American educators have considered that schools would be out of bounds if they took up this takes of building values. The result is our national society presents a picture of something short of moral stamina.

Leaders in the progressive movement, notably Kilpatrick and Childs, while nothing the challenge of social change for the curriculum, originally placed their faith in the continuous reconstruction of experience,[17] and stated the need for a "society composed of people who can creatively find their controlling ideas and ideals in the on-going process of experience itself."[18] They thought education should emphasize a method for achieving a dynamic society. It should provide the learner with the society of the scientific method for controlling observations, experimentations, development of hypotheses, and testing through experience. It was assumed that learning to work under such conditions of scientific control would develop desirable values in each generation of learners which would accrue to the benefit of humanity. However, progressive education had such a limited trial, no general conclusions, pro or con, are possible relative to this proposition. In the later works of John Dewey and John L. Childs there appear to be modifications of original views on the role of adult determined values in education. Here both men have demonstrated the importance of value systems laboriously built up by the culture over the years. Experience has proven the validity, they say, of certain of our common social values.[19]

Counts piaces his confidence in American education to take the best of this nation's moral and social values and forage a truly American ideology.[20] Curriculum activities would be direct toward the fulfilment of the values and principles of this ideology. No teacher could ever feel in this scheme of things that his job was unimportant. The profession of teaching would then have a substantial significance in the society beyond that which is now enjoys. This nation, principally through its educational system, could at least find out what it is truly capable of in this continent and in its relationship to the world. It could inspire its citizens, its teachers, and its students of unimagined levels of creativity in the process toward social and psychological maturity.

Yet, American education is not equal to this task at present Counts says:

Although we have developed a good education, an education of which we can rightly be proud, we have never developed a truly great education, an education which expresses the best of our heritage. We have lived below the possibilities of our civilization.[21]

Like Sorokin, Counts speaks of the great unrealized moral commitments of our American civilization, the make-up of which insure a continuous dynamism of our national life if seriously applied. There are: (1) the ethics of the Judeo-Christian tradition, (2) the humanistic spirit, (3) the scientific method, (4) the democratic process, and (5) the cause of world peace.[22] These values, meanings, and principles make up the best of America's potential ideology. In no period of history has such an ideology been effectively actualized in a society through man's behavior. If it were, it would by no means produce a static society; indeed, it is open-ended to the future and its creative possibilities would never be exhausted.

Implications for Behavioral Change

The democratic process and the scientific method are at once ideological and behavioral. In the case of each a course of action is assured. The problem of developing a behavioral component which can truly translate into action the American ideology, will result from the development by the educator of curricular methods and teaching-learning situations which embody democratic process and the scientific method of problem-solving. Democracy makes use of the Judeo-Christian ethics and the humanistic spirit, and thus it incorporates much that the American ideology calls for. If true democracy could be developed in all institutions and societies in the world, there can be no doubt that this would be the greatest possible step toward universal peace.

The progressive education movement placed its faith in methods with the expectation that those methods would inevitably produce social values of worth to the child and to the society. That methods of procedure have crucial effects on the total learning cannot be denied. Many valuable methods have been devised by the progressive movement. Not only do the integrative methods developed by this movement promote more complex learning outcomes while sacrificing none of the basic skills, but these methods employ the scientific method and the democratic process as their rationale for learning. No group of thinkers before in the history of education has given more thought to the development of these twin processes; however, the progressivists tended to rely too heavily on the probability of the emerging democratic values and processes in contrast to the intelligent guidance of their growth. The role of the teacher in deliberately setting up process for desired ends should never be abrogated. Methods should never be considered learning in toto.

Educational methodology should become highly dynamic. Whatever methods allow for the greatest quantity and quality of human interaction, these are likely to be the most creative. Singular methods should go into limbo. Methods should change with the situation and with the dynamic content of American life. Methods will maintain a high degree of correlation under a more slowly changing ideology. There will be, always, a great distances between the actual behaviour of the people and the adopted ideology; therefore, new ways of approaching the goals should be involved constantly. Probable no ideal set of methods will ever be settled upon. As teachers and students work through new methods of achieving their goals, the refinement of the ideology, in turn, is inevitable.

The behavioral component, in constant interaction with the ideological component and the material component, will have its peculiar effect upon changes in the total culture as well. Social inventions tried and tested in the schools will take their place in the total structure of society, replacing methods which either no longer articulate the prevailing ideology or which do not articulate it as well as new.

The culture can become crystallized in methodology, and the same is true for the curriculum. The authoritarian curriculum of the American school is a most obvious example of practices which have persisted in very much the same form for centuries. The subject-centered curriculum takes very little notice of the present dynamic culture. Its subjects were created to meet the original needs of a changing world, but that purpose has now often disappeared. Often retained because of intertia, these subjects have developed a questionable respectability under the guise of "mental discipline" or "transfer of training." Crystallization of curriculum can be effectively prevented by constantly devising a variety of methods and activities for achieving learning which in turn constantly refines ideology and materials.

Implications for Material Change

Our nation has, potentially and actually, the best material component of any social system known or imagined. Because of the imbalance between the ideological and the behavioral components, the material culture has tended to dominate American life. Change in the former along the lines recommended above would not adversely affect the material wealth and prosperity of the nation although, admittedly, our material giantism is partly a result of strong materialistic values among our people. In the new education, ways will be discovered to use the material component in the achievement of greater human happiness.

The precept "altering the field alters the child" is as true for the material setting for learning as for any other component. Both society and the curriculum will be changed by improved tools, vehicles, buildings, teaching aids, etc. It is a well-known fact that slums, by their very material setting, breed crime and disease.

Attention to the type of school buildings and classrooms to be built may yield some productive results. The progressivists have already produced some significant in the physical setting for learning. School buildings are more functional and less ornate than in the past. Classrooms are closer to the out-of-doors. Modern arrangement of furniture and materials in the classroom facilitates group activities and problem-solving. More and different kinds of books and instructional supplies help learners become discriminating and self-directing in their voyages of discovery in the learning process. The classroom of the progressive school is quite different from the stern and forbidding setting of yesterday with its rigid rows of seats. In such a setting, it is now wonder that there were few compelling peer relationships or that verbalisms became the chief learning mechanism.

The material component of education is open vast improvement, experimentation, and development. If the tremendous technological already amassed by our culture could be applied to matters of education in a major way, there can be no doubt that important changes would occur in the curriculum. Students of tomorrow should be introduced early into the actual tools of living because of the rapidity and the acceleration of the change which Ogburn, as quoted previously, thinks will pervade their time. Students will have increasingly more to learn. The material setting will have to be moved closer to the real life of the total culture. Formal subjects may have to give way to guided experiences in the factories, on the farms, in the laboratories, in the streams of commerce, in the social agencies and the like. Education will have to become less and less artificial and more and more a genuine part of the on-going life of the culture itself. In short, the materials of the learning process will have to become the actual tools of everyday living.

SUMMARY

As the teacher surveys the present situation in the world with its acure strain in social processes and the almost constant threat of open war painted against an enduring backdrop of cold war, he may well feel a sense of almost utter futility. Although men have dreamed of "one world," the world has never achieved this wholeness. Every age has been an age out of point. It is incorrect unfortunately, to speak of a "world community." The United Nations is not an integral, world society, though one would hope that eventually it become so. It cannot function effectively until a much great number of men and of nations accept mutual, or at least similar, working values and behaviors. This can come to pass only through social change. Social change is the only way to move toward maturity in interpersonal, community, national, or international relations. At the very base of it all is a particular kind of social change—*curriculum change.* How shall we achieve this dream of a changed, better world except throughout education, a changed, better education?

The key component which educators must concentrate upon for effective curriculum improvement is the *behavioral* component. For change in people and their ways of doing thing is the greatest need of the hour. Curriculum change can contribute much to change in the total culture when it concentrates upon changed behaviors in the rising generation.

SELECTED READINGS

Brameld, Theodore, *Philosophies of Education in Cultural Perspective,* New York, Dryden Press, Inc., 1955, Chap. 4, 5, & 6.

Lerner, Max,. *America As a Civilization,* New York, Simon and Schuster, Inc., 1957, Chapter. 2, 4 & 12.

Sorokin, Pitirim A., *Society Cultural and Personality,* New York, Harper & Bros., 1947, Chaps. 17, 45, & 46.

Wish, Harvey, *Society and Thought in Modern America,* New York, Longmans, Green & Co., 1952, Chaps. 22, 23 & 24.

REFERENCES

1. Theodore Brameld, *Philosophers of Education in Cultural Perspective*, New York, Dryden Press, Inc, 1955, p. 388
2. Harold Rugg, *Curriculum Making. Past and Present,* Part I, Bloomington, III, Public School Publishing Co., 1926, p. 3.
3. Lloyd Allen Cook, *Community Backgrounds of Education,* New York McGraw Hill Book Co., 1938, pp. 1-2.
4. Alice Miel, *Changing the Curriculum,* New York, Appleton-Century-Crofts, Inc., 1946, p. 11.
5. Pitirim A. Sorokin, *Society, Culture* and *Personality,* New York, Harper & Bros. 1947, pp. 41-42.
6. William F. Ogburn, *Social Change*, New York, B.W. Huebsch, Inc., 1922, pp. 200-201.
7. William F. Ogburn and Meyer F. Nimkoff, *Sociology,* 2nd ed., New York, Houghton Mifflin Co., 1950, pp. 550-551.
8. *Ibid.,* pp. 847-855
9. Robert M. MacIver, *Society,* New York, Rinehart & Co., 1937, p. 395.
10. *Ibid.,* pp. 409-415
11. Pitirim A. Sorokin, *Contemporary Sociological Theories.* New York Harper & Bros. 1928, pp. 744-745.
12. Pitirim A. Sorokin, *Society, Cultural and Personality,* New York, Harper & Bros., 1947, pp. 41-42.
13. *Ibid.,* pp. 380-381.
14. *Ibid.,* pp. 555-556.
15. *Ibid.,* pp. 696 697.
16. *Ibid.,* pp. 508-08
17. William Heard Kilpatrick, *Education for a Changing Civilization,* New York, The Macmillan Co., 1929, p. 123.
18. John L. Childs, *Education and the Philosophy of Experimentalism.* New York, Century Publishing Co., 1931, p. 133.
19. John Dewey, *A Common Faith* New Haven, Conn., Yale University Press, 1934, pp. 44-52; John L., Childs, *Education and Morals* New York, Appleton-Century-Crofts, Inc., 1950, pp. 1-38.
20. George S. Counts, *Education and the Promise of America,* New York, The Macmillan Co., 1945 pp. 104-105.
21. *Ibid.,* p. 19.
22. *Ibid.,* pp. 77-98.

4

CURRICULUM IMPROVEMENT PROGRAMS

Participation in cooperative curriculum programs to improve the learning situation for children is an integral, highly important part of the work of the professional teacher and administrator. Just as important is the participation of parents, other laymen in the community, and, of course the children themselves. Cooperative programs for curriculum improvement must be interactive with the daily curriculum development of the classroom if any real success is to be attained. It is unnecessary to remind most school people today that curriculum development really takes place when teachers and pupils undertake to learn, in the classroom or wherever the learning situation takes them.

With this concept of curriculum development governing our thinking, the most distinctly professional behaviour of teachers is constant study, evaluation, and experimentation to aid learners in their quests, just as research and laboratory work in the medical field leads to and emerges from the treatment of patients. As in the medical field, this work cannot be left entreaty to individual initiative or to accident. Much help can be rendered the teacher through cooperative efforts, through group problem solving, and through special services. It is important to analyse, profiting from the mistakes of the past, how the cooperative approach to curriculum development can be effectively organized and led.

PRINCIPLES GOVERNING CURRICULUM IMPROVEMENT PROGRAMS

1. To Change People Through Problem Solving and Democratic Action

During the past half century school personnel have poured a

prodigious amount of time and energy into large-scale, cooperative curriculum improvement programs that typically have resulted in only superficial improvements in the curriculum of the elementary school. The regular failure of such programs to achieve creditable success has been a matter of grave concern to leadig thinkers during the past decade, among them Stephen Corey, who says: " A major difficulty with cooperative curriculum development, of course, is that while the process is relatively easy to describe, very few of us have learned the attitudes, the skills, the values, and the information that are required if this method of improving a school program is to have any chance of succeeding."[1]

Too many of such programs apparently have concentrated upon quickly drawing up paper changes to justify the time and money spent by school systems and profession personnel. An example of such "paper" programs can be seen in the rather widespread practice of attempting to initiate curriculum program by encouraging teacher-groups to write extended lists of instruction objectives. Too often, these written lists of objectives have been field away and almost forgotten because such statements are most likely to be abstract and far removed from the realities of classroom practice.[2] During the time-consuming process of listing abstract objectives which were supposed to indicate the directions the whole curriculum project was to take, the present problems of the teaching-learning situation were bypassed. The popular saying among many school people that, "We can't go anywhere until we know *where* we are going," should be examined. This is certainly not characteristic of a scientific problem solving attitude. The scientific investigator is not absorbed with where his investigation is taking him but rather in attending on the immediate problem and in developing possible solutions. The preoccupation with objectives, then prevents us from focusing upon our real problems. Curriculum problems invariably involve what people are doing with processes. Curriculum change is, primarily, change in teachers and their ways of doing things. The traditional practice of listing instructional objectives relegates to the background the main purpose of cooperative problem-solving namely, changes in the people involve themselves.[3] Democratic process in curriculum programs should not have to be justified in a democratic society. If the school is to assume its obligation to develop citizens who will participate to the fullest in the democratic process of society, then, of necessity, it must function as an effective example of democratic procedure. Teachers cannot be expected to develop democratic process in their classrooms if their own professional relationships are governed by authoritarian or laissez faire attitudes and procedures. One of the chief results of democratically organized curriculum programs should be the growth of democratically functioning personalities among teachers and administrators. These personalities, too, will have a direct effect on children in the classroom.

Every person needs to be independent respected and self-respecting, and to have statues and wholesome interactive relations with other individuals in a social group. Problem-entered group process furnishes the operational setting in which these needs can be met. These human relationships make possible the fusing of separate and unique individuals into a social group capable of thinking and working toward a common goal, the solution of a common problem. The problem might impinge upon individuals in different ways and degrees and each individual always has his own unique objective; yet, there are enough universal in the problem situation to bind them together as a unit. The mistake many group leaders make is trying to develop uniformity of thinking and response to the problem. Individual expression and creativity within the plan for group organization and focus is essential. Given satisfactory interaction and reciprocal relations within the group, the process develops among participants a wholesome morale a feeling of "we" and of belonging, and an enthusiasm for cooperative enterprise. The individual, acting on impetus from the energies built up in the group effort to solve a problem, of his own validation continues, apart from the group, to direct his activities toward the problem's solution.[4]

Original ideas will surface from the great pool of thinking going on in the interactive process. Few ideas can be imposed successfully upon the group from the outside.[5] The group seems to prefer its own intellectual resources. Contributions to the intellectual exchange, like those of a child in the classroom, help the individual to achieve some feeling of status. The group members prove to each other the old adage that two heads (or multiples thereof) are better than one when they work together toward common goals. As they exchange ideas on a reciprocal basis, they tend to take on the characteristics of a social organism: self-sufficiency, resistance to outside interferences, oneness of purpose, loyalty.

II. To Initiate and Control Conditions Favourable to Curriculum Change

Deep changes can occur only in a person willingly seeking to be different. The desire for change must come from within the individual himself. On the other hand, once the scene and climate for change have established, some change in individuals can be expected as inevitable. Administration fulfils its function on a high place when it provides the conditions necessary for a teacher to become happier, more successful, more secure person, in turn a better leader of children. Of course, this cannot be accomplished by making all the decisions for that teacher, by formulating a rigid routine, or by reducing the need for change. On the other hand, the knowledge that change and inventiveness are not only permitted but even encouraged will make the normal person function as a happier, more complete personality. Given this attitude by an administrator, a faculty will strive to improve, and curriculum change will move with decisiveness. Therefore the most effective administrator does not attempt to prescribe for teachers. He may tell them what he thinks at the appropriate time in group problem-solving, but he does not expect them to follow his advice simply because he has the status of leader. He may insist that they hear and consider all alternatives, including his own, before acting, but when the administrator can see his own solution by-passed by the group and not feel loss of face, he is a democratic leader.

The cooperative curriculum development program cannot be the pet scheme of any one person. It is concerned with improvement of the total teaching-learning situation. It should involve all personnel, and each person should have a voice in the directions to be taken. Yesterday's administrator thought of the training of the teacher in-service. Today, he ponders his role as a leader whose chief function is to stimulate professional growth through cooerative means and to coordinate the efforts of all. Instead of concentrating on telling or showing teachers how to do their work better, the supervisor or principal leads them in the analysis and evaluation of the total teaching-learning situation so that the whole professional community might find out how to improve that situation. The professional growth to the individual, then, is bound up with the improvement of the total curriculum. Leaders should help teachers where possible, to see themselves realistically, to diagnose learning situations in which they are involved, and to develop the habit of searching for better answers.

As the educational leader works with teachers, pupils, and parents in curriculum planning, he helps to provide the know-how coordinates plans for use of resources, schedules activities secures needed consultative help, encourages the active participation of many people in the development of goals and the ways to achieve them, and encourages their continuous evaluation of those goals and methods. This is a necessary status role of dignity and respect, year democratic and nonauthoritarian.

The administrator must know what effective teaching is, and recognize that there are many different kinds of effective teaching. He should know and understand the growth and development of children. He can be of immense value to a group if he is constantly on the look-out for new materials and for ways to employ his special competencies to aid the group in pushing its program forward.

Some administrators to aid the group in pushing its program order to appear favourably in the eyes of the lay public and to maintain control over teachers and pupils. As democratic leaders, however, they soon learn these assumptions are false. The highest place is reserved for an enthusiastic and dynamic leader who can inspire others to greater effort. It is leadership and not dictation that elicits maximum efforts.

When a teacher recognizes a problem and appears eager to seek new answers, the administrator is presented with an opportunity to cultivate creativity, self-direction, and extra effort. He should approach the opportunity with enthusiasm, lending encouragement and providing resources as far as possible. He should work with a group in the same way, realizing however that there can hardly ever be one focus of interests among a group of teachers. He will help the group organize so that the varied interests and needs of all will be accommodated sooner or later in the process of curriculum improvement. He may require all staff members to take part in some aspect of curriculum development but he will recognize that each individual should be encouraged to work on problems which interest him. An initial step for him will be an awareness of what his teachers' own recognizable problems are. Under such leadership, teachers will tend to live up to what is confidently expected of them. Once caught up in the deliberative group process or in their own action research they will extend themselves beyond their own preliminary or immediate objectives.

While considering how to enrich the materials and resources of the curriculum the principal and teachers should look to parents and to the physical social and industrial resources of the community. Rich learning experiences, for more children, will result if all the teachers in a school unit plan together and cooperate in the use of these materials and resources.

One of the most beneficial experiences for a faculty ensues when an administrator arranges visits to other schools. When teachers interact with other teachers who are in another situation, especially at the same grade level, stimulating ideas are often exchanged. They find they have, or have had, similar problems, and, by sharing their experiences and solutions, they often arrive at a newer, more professional level of thinking about them. After the visitations the cooperative pooling of ideas and suggestions brings to light many new answers for the local situation.

Few teachers will engage in action research if there is a feeling of insecurity or fear. Teachers must feel that their principal and supervisors understand what they are trying to do and approve of their efforts. Only in a climate of freedom, then, will faculties be released to participate in curriculum development endeavours at their highest pitch, to concentrate in the best interests of learners, undeterred by worries concerning the security of their employment.

The one-to-one relationship of administrator to teacher is not the only area for consideration of how the climate of feeling surrounding the teacher may be improved. The principal and supervisor are responsible, also, for the encouragement and intelligent guidance of genuine cooperation among teachers, for the group itself conditions, to a considerable extent, the actions and the feelings of each member. In fact, throughout the school environment every person who in any way contacts the pupil or the teacher has a definite influence on the climate of the classroom. Therefore an important job of the status leader is, through all means available, to improve the human relation among all participants of a curriculum development program.

The leader establishes the psychological bases of staff morale by providing an atmosphere of responsible freedom and approval by informing teachers of what may be reasonably expected of them by the school board and other authorities and by behaving consistently in his relationship with all concerned. The need for self-realization by teachers can be partially met by stimulating them to participate in formulating policy and by assuming significant responsibilities. Another area of concern for the administrator is the elimination of unnecessary teacher anxieties. As Bushong says: "The modern school administrator soon learns that his staff cannot function at its best if the horizon is overcast with fears, doubt and suspicion.... By building a good working climate on the foundation of trust, sincerity and mutual respect, the leader can lay to rest many nameless anxieties of the staff."[6]

If the teacher is the central figure in the developments of classroom climate, surely the administrator is the critical factor in the emotional climate within which the teachers work. Adults, like children, desire social approval and identification with a group. Teachers also reflect, in their estimates of themselves, the kinds of treatment they receive from administrators, colleagues, and the parents of the pupils. Positive action will be hindered by the communication of unhealthy emotions in interpersonal relationships.[7]

III. To Stimulate Action Research at the Classroom Level by Giving Sanction, Status, and Assistance to Teachers

Administrators, curriculum directors, and curriculum councils often have approached curriculum improvement programs for a school system with mass meetings, the compilation of instructional objectives by teacher groups, or discussion "buzz" groups. The dilemma in such approaches usually is that either administrators will appear to dictate a predetermined program, or an ill-prepared group will flounder in confusion. Invariably, individual teachers feel that the initiative and responsibility for action lies with administrators after attending such meetings. At best, teachers return to their classrooms believing the curriculum program to be some what remote from, their working world.

Group discussion and planning can be a far richer experience when the concrete results for action research can be shared. For it is often remarked that discussion leads nowhere when participants are pooling ignorance and gossip. Since curriculum change cannot be dictated by the status leaders, and group discussion often proves fruitless when staff members start "cold," action research project offer a problem solving situation. Supervisors and administrators should encourage and assist individual teachers in solving their own problems through action research projects established within the problems through action research projects established within the framework of the total design of the school's curriculum, school policy, and the resources available.

What is action research? In any mode, research on the curriculum is difficult. Like the social process and personality, the curriculum process is so complex, it does not lend itself readily to narrow focus or structural analysis of parts. Formal research in the curricular components can lead to distorted findings. Even the clear findings of formal research in a skill area, for instance, may be inoperable in the larger matrix of the school program. Moreover, formal research requires a special set of conditions which seldom can be devised in the everyday work of the school. Action research, on the other hand, can be used directly with the on-going curricular development and change itself. If a teacher is plagued by doubts concerning something he is doing and considers "What would happen if I tried something different?" That teacher is ripe for action research. Carrying out that something to see if it will work is action research. Action research, then, is improvement of the teaching-learning situation on the job. It places emphasis upon practical experimentation and problem-solving as the teacher meets the children in the learning situation.

The primary outcome of action research is the changes in the people who engage in it. The changes take the form of new insight, new understanding, new techniques, new feelings, etc., which are personal growth in the individuals involved. Other results may be derived from other's knowledge of the experiment and its results. Such knowledge may lead others more quickly in their own direct experience and to proceed with fewer mistakes. Therefore the reports of action research are as those of formal research. Keeping informal records, making periodic observations, giving tests, developing reports on special subjects affected by the experimentation—all help the teacher to better understand what the research situation is accomplishing and give to the teacher the objective kinds of data which can be communicated to others.

Teachers and pupils are partners in the learning experiences controlled by action research. The teaching program does not suffer; to the contrary, action research itself is a method proven many times to be highly successful in promoting learning. It places everyone concerned in scientific frame of reference. Valuable attitudes and skills can be immediate rewards for pupils as well as teachers.

Administrators should provide for the sharing of action research projects in process and upon culmination. These projects may appear, at first, to be isolated and separate studies but leadership can, over a period of time, recognize those which seem to be promising and call attention to them, provide for teacher visitation, or specific reports. Teachers in these separate patterns of action research will share and grow, then, in situations created by supervision and administration. As the projects mature under the guidance of curriculum leaders, specialists, and various kinds of consultants, the separate identities of the projects will become secondary as common, helpful elements emerge and are accepted in general practice.

IV. To Compile Curriculum Records to Share What Has Already Happened

Action research that seeks new answers in the process of curriculum change net always be always be recorded in writing. Often, however, It is valuable to a teacher's associates and to the professional word to receive a report of the project. As in the case of formal experimentation, the solutions can be recorded only after the *experience* of research. Teachers may profit somewhat by recording tentative hypotheses or listing questions to be explored; but the old habit of compiling long lists of instructional objectives is totally unprofitable. If anyone should desire to engage in such an activity in connection with curriculum projects, lists of such objectives written during the past half century are available for thousands of courses of study. These objectives, however, have been written too often by people with a narrow academic orientation who appear best solely on raising another set of graded standards for a heterogeneous population to hurdle as a group. Blind to the natural and differentiated characteristics of children with their great range in abilities, these tiresome products of many a past curriculum project tend to pull teaching down from the level of professional competence and respect.

What intelligent teachers really would study for help in the teaching-learning situation are:

1. Logs of unusual experiences by learners giving the operational steps and narrative events of projects.
2. Learning materials used in particular experiences, their cost, and their sources.
3. Drawing or pictures of apparatus and construction products, their patterns, measurements, and operational characteristics.
4. Bulletin board ideas.
5. Case studies of "problem children" complete with expert interpretation and recommendations for action.
6. Review of instructional films by teachers who work on the same level as themselves.
7. Write-ups of science experiments with explanation of why the demonstrations may not work as expected.
8. Typical results which may be expected of children in various units of work in terms of their mental ages.
9. Novel ways of introducing pupils to children's literature.

This is an incomplete list. The type of items in it suggest what is really helpful to write down about the curriculum. The neat and carefully drawn course study for a particular grade becomes increasingly less useful to the practical teacher who is learning to teach children in terms of their individual readiness and maturity. The subject matter objectives of a course of study for Grade 4, for example, will be applicable to only a fraction of the pupils in Grade 4, and not all of these at the same time. For many teachers, the implication has been that all children of a grade group were to cover the material of the course of study for that grade, and if they could not do so, they did not belong in that grade. Where such a concept to teaching prevailed, the able pupil too often was held back to the pace of the class. Doubtless, then, rigid adherence to the course of study for all children has given justification to some critics of American education who declare that instruction is "pitched to the mediocre."

The detailed course of study also carries with it the implication that the subject matter and experiences described in it will be imposed systematically on the learners, and as a result, the rationale in the typical elementary school classroom of the nation has remained authoritarian and autocratic despite significant evidence a democratic, problem-solving curriculum is best for optimum developments and mental health. Nothing appears more obstructive to the development of such a curriculum than writing about and adherence to graded courses of study. Curriculum improvement programs which are based on this system and on these products, however, engender a significantly different psychological climate for curriculum planning. Opportunities for genuine teacher growth are necessarily limited by the process.

Reporting experiences in curriculum development, then, is the final phase of a curriculum improvement project. Naturally, this writing should not take the form of courses of study which duplicate, in the main textual materials, but rather, it should report action research and the suggestions for procedure which come from significant and rewarding experiences in the classroom. When the curriculum is perceived as that which goes on each moment in the learning situation and that the story of the curriculum in any particular classroom cannot be written down in advance, then school systems will recognize that curriculum improvement program are continuous and integral with the on-going curriculum of the teaching-learning situation, is the research and laboratory work of the physician relate to the patient and his treatment. This will mean that administrators and teachers will place their faith in, and expend their effort toward, significant change in people rather than changes in their paper work.

THE DELTA COUNTY CURRICULUM PROJECT

Perhaps too few curriculum studies have focused on the mental hygiene point of view derived from recent knowledge in the behavioural science.[8] Moreover, too few curriculum studies have utilized the process of action research, a process in which people study problems real to them in their usual on-the-job situation and in which the primary results are change in these same people and their ways doing things. The teaching, supervisory, and administrative staffs of the four rural school systems of Delta County, Texas, recently complete a three-year action research study of their curricula which had as its major aim the focusing of the total school program on mental hygiene.

The faculties of the four school systems of Delta County in meetings of their local teacher association decided to undertake a study of their existing school curricula and facilities in the fall of 1952. A steering committee consisting of the county school superintendent, the county school supervisor, the four local school superintendents and one classroom teacher from each of the four divisions—primary, intermediate, junior high school, senior high school—met to plan the project and to obtain a consultant. The committee contacted the texas Education Agency and the Hogg Foundation for Mental Hygiene for advice and assistance. By mid-November, the group had received a tentative promise of financial assistance from the Hogg Foundation and a promise of consultative help from the Texas Education Agency for at least the initial phase of the study. The steering committee made contact with East Texas State Teachers College for the services of a resident consultant since all of the school concerned lay within twenty-five miles of that institution. By early December, the committee, the consultant, the Texas Education Agency, and the Hogg Foundation has played a role in the group deliberations, and the way was paved for mass involvement of all professional personnel.

During the first month, the consultant spent considerable time in each classroom of all the school involved in the study of orient himself regarding the existing practices, resources and facilities, and to meet each staff member personally on the job. He encouraged teachers to visit each other in classroom situations both in the same system and in other in classroom situations both in the same system and in other systems. The steering committee set a schedule to facilitate these visitations, and the superintendents of the various schools released the touchers from the regular school day for the visits. Since the four systems had decided to work together cooperatively in the project, the intervisitation of teachers helped the individuals to know each other better and to exchange ideas. Changes in the teacher and their ways of doing things began, noticeably, at this time.

During the early months of the project, the consultant and guest speakers obtained either by the steering committee or by the consultant, made several presentations to the group of information on the nature of action research, and recent research findings in the fields of mental hygiene, psychology of learning, and curriculum development. These presentations stimulated general discussions in which teachers' questions and problems relating to their existing classroom situation increasingly took the centre of interest. The consultant arranged for a problem inventory the formation of work groups on the various grade levels, and an investigation of the professional literature on problems of interest to each group.

This phase of the project led to a significant and hoped for development—an expression by several teachers of the desire to experiment with new methods and techniques in their own classroom. Interaction between the study groups and the action research going on in classrooms became commonplace, the one contributing importantly to the other.

The consultant and the county elementary supervisor helped teachers get their experimental projects under way and furnished guidance to sustain them. These action research projects took various forms. Some teachers wanted to organize children in democratic and problem-solving activities in a unit of work; others were concerned with getting immediately to some of the individual problems of their children and chose to develop case studies; other projects involved sociometrical techniques field trips, planning and carrying out the landscaping of the school grounds, free expression art projects, and group guidance. Teachers who saw relation among these types of activities found it desirable to combine several in their classroom programs. Often one type of activity grew into another.

The teachers expressed a need for constant help from the consultant and other persons who had experience with the techniques and ways of working involved in this method of curriculum study. They found some security and real help in exchanging ideas and experience with their fellow teacher in their own and in other school systems of the four cooperating districts. For this purpose, frequent small group meetings were called to discuss a particular problem. General meeting of the combined staffs were held once monthly during the entire project. Not only could teachers enjoy the satisfaction of group planning, experimentation, are reporting, but also the individual teacher often expressed the pleasure and satisfaction of personal growth. The consultant and other leaders in the group constantly exploited opportunities in both school and community situations to call attention to the success of individuals. The individuals, in turn, often expressed appreciation for the climate furnished by the various administrators in which experimentation was encouraged.

Not all was satisfactory, however. It was difficult to make the study cooperative, especially among the school systems. Progress was not even, and sometimes it was lost for lack of effective consolidation. Teachers spent considerable time in studying children and in collecting data of all sorts relating to their classroom experimentation, and yet, it was difficult to find time to record behaviour accurately, to administer and score tests, and to use the various scales and techniques which were developed. Moreover, the "community school" concept, as it developed, took more and more of the extra-class time of teachers. Keeping an "eye on the ball" or their major objective was not easy. Loss of perspective often led to confusion and discouragement. The idea of action research, nevertheless, triumphed. The over burdened teacher was much more willing to undertake an in-service professional study contributing directly to his classroom situation. Finding time to carry on even this type of study was a problem, but pleasure was expressed over the definite help given the teacher in the solution of problems during the ordinary course of classroom work.

Scope and Sequence Study

In addition to the experimentation in curriculum design, teaching techniques, and guidance by teachers, the Delta County group undertook a study of the efficacy of rural education in general from Grade 1 to high school graduation, and the role of the small rural high school in particular. Problems relating to the limited materials available in small school systems the appropriateness of a formal curriculum for a rural region, the apparent lack of justification for the existing scope and sequence and related questions led the group during the early months of the study's first year to a general analysis of the scope for each grade level and how the work of each grade contributed to the total sequence. It became apparent that there was no recognizable scope for some of the levels. Scope and sequence was determined, if at all, by the particular textbooks in use. The group decided to work out a scope and sequence without regard necessarily to the available textbooks but, rather with the considerations of child development, mental health principles, needs of modern society, and needs of their own rural region in mind. The group then formulated a new program, the framework of which is represented by the following:

Grade 1: Living Together at Home and at School

Grade 2: Living Together in Our Neighbourhood

Grade 3: Living Together in Our Larger Community

Grade 4: Living Together in Our State

Grade 5: Living Together in the United States

Grade 6: Living Together in the Americas

Grade 7: Living Together in One World

Grade 8: Understanding Ourselves and Others

Grade 9: Understanding the Problem and Potentialities of our State

Grade 10: Understanding Our American Democracy

Grade 11: Understanding Our Economic and Technolocial Culture

Grade 12: Understanding Present and Past Efforts Toward World Cooperation and Universal Peace.

Units and projects were tried out during the three years of the study at each grade level, in terms of the theme for each grade, as indicated above. Gradually the units, projects or other outlines which represented the development of a comprehensive teaching program for each took form and were bound into curriculum guides.

The grade themes in themselves reflected desirable concepts of mutual cooperation among people and of the importance of facing the realities of a modern world in the process of rapid change. This mental hygiene framework for a curriculum was complemented by problem-solving units such as: "How We Work and play Together at School in the first few weeks of a first-grade term, "How We Can Understand Better Our Parents and Other Adults in the Community" in Grade 8. "How Democracy Work in Everyday Living" in Grade 10, and "How Men Have Struggled to Build Up a Universal Code of Law" in Grade

12. Each unit contributed to the general concept expressed in the theme or scope for that grade.

This program was carried on in self-contained classroom in Grade 1 through 6 and can be described as an integrated program supplemented by systematic teaching in the skill areas. In Grades 7 through 12, this program was organized as a *Core* involving approximately half of the school day in two of the high school. In the other two high schools, topics related to the grade themes were introduced into the regular courses wherever possible and into the assembly and club programs. Methods of learning by students changed significantly in the former; no changes appeared in the latter.

Statement of Purposes

Like most teachers, supervisors, and administrators, the faculties of the Delta County schools were familiar with the several comprehensive statements of educational objectives available to the profession like that of the Educational Policies Commission. The group never felt a need to revise such comprehensive statements. However, as reading, study, experimentation, and discussion went forward within the group, especially in the more unfamiliar area of mental hygiene, the group bean to grope for generalizations which could express the meaning of action research based on mental health and thereby improve the communication and thinking of members of the group. This development came to fruition near the end of the first year of the study in a preliminary draft of purposes. This draft was almost continuously revised until the end of the study and the final statement was as follows:

A curriculum focused on mental hygiene should:

1. Provide daily experiences in democratic living which help each child to gain status or a feeling of belonging in his group and in his community.
2. Provide situations daily in which each child can enjoy feeling of success or achievement in terms of his own potentialities of group goals.
3. Provide situations daily in which each child gains new and challenging experiences.

4. Provide a climate of feeling in human relationship which help each child to grow in emotional security.
5. Provide for the purposeful and functional, acquisition of the tools or basic skills essential to effective-living i today's world.
6. Provide for a rich contact with the accumulating cultural heritage in the solving of present problems and in the pursuit of leisure.
7. Provide experiences demonstrating how science and democracy promote constructive change through problem-solving and group deliberation, and how our American ideals are so high, we always move forward.

It appeared to the consultant that this statement of purposes resulted in the first genuine feeling of solidarity in the countywide group. It became more than a message to themselves on the daily job; it became also a message to the world by a group dedicated anew to the mission of education in a free society.

Developmental Highlights of Project

Behind the statement of purposes, as developed over the three-year period, there were a number of critical events, new insights, and results of experimentation and study which might be beneficial. Maximum interest probably will be served by an analysis of the thinking the actions, as much as by the actions themselves, Experience proved to the consultant that new techniques tried out merely upon suggestion by another are seldom successful or enduring. On the other hand, teacher who had a problem to solve and made a real effort to study and think through the "why" back of the technique utilized usually fond the technique successful. On the basis of a number of needs felt among teachers, a study program was instituted parallel with classroom experimentation.

References to status or the feeling of belonging in the professional literature and in presentations to the group provoked interest in the work groups. A relationship between democratic values in group process and the opportunities for the development of the feeling of belonging became apparent. The experiments of Kurt Lewin and associates[9] in "social climates" were reviewed. Democracy was found to be the climate suited to the development of mental health in general and to the development of belonging and group solidarity in particular, whereas autocratic and laissez faire social climates tended to cultivate egocentricity and forms of aggression. Hostility and tension among members of the group were found to have emerged especially in the autocratic climate. Since most of the teaching in Delta County schools was admittedly of the autocratic or authoritarian type, this information appeared to make a profound impression among the teachers. They noted other implications of democracy for constructive classroom work. For example, democratic groups are more stable in structure, more objective in evaluation or interpretation of events, more inclined to have a feeling of "we." more inclined to choose cooperative rather than individual endeavours, less likely to involve personal feelings in the give-and-take of discussion or criticism, more inclined to develop constructive and sustained work habits, and more likely to develop a feeling for group property and group goals.

Still trying to understand the full significance of the feeling of belonging in the classroom, teachers reviewed several methods and techniques advocated in the professional literature, among them the unit or project method and the sociogram. The unit method was acclaimed for having democratic and problem-solving processes which provide a satisfying role for every child to play in achieving the goals of group endeavor. Further, heterogeneous grouping was held to be an advantage in a democratic situation which placed great worth on each child in his own right and as a group member. Each child was seen to contribute in his own unique way to the needs of the group, and through these unique contributions received recognition from the group as a worthwhile member. The relationship between the process of achieving status in a group by children in their own classroom and the data which teachers secured from applying the sociogram technique led to new insights, and led, in turn, to the development of the case study technique of children who appeared to be social isolates. Group problem-solving appeared to meet individual differences through utilizing those very differences to advantage in the typically differentiated tasks of the process.

Finding that individual differences in a class constituted a blessing rather than a curse in the unit method of teaching, the Delta County teachers wanted to know more about those differences. They found that random group 6-year-old children in a typical first-grade class will exhibit a range of more than four year in mental age and in such specific reading or number readiness. Further, it was found that these same children on reaching Grade 7 will exhibit a range of about eight years in mental age and most achievement areas, and that one could expect the range of differences to increase steadily with growth and education.[10] Although the professional school people of Delta County had heard the term "individual differences" many times, the facts about them were difficult to believe. This information led to a comprehensive testing program in the four school systems and an analysis of the data on their own children.

One of the early consequences of the testing program was the location of children who needed special help. Concurrently, the teachers were gaining information on developing in their pupils the feeling of success or mastery. They concluded that the mass assignments, the mass tests, and the comparative marking system used were condemning too many children to daily failures and inevitable frustrations. They recognized that these sustained failures left many children defeated often unwilling to try. They saw the American school contributing unwittingly to feelings of inadequacy and hostility instead of concerning itself with the development of feelings of success, mastery, or adequacy within each child every day. Further, they concluded that the curriculum should act to rescue the child from unfair competitive situations in which success is impossible and to place him in cooperative situations in which unique can be utilized to best advantage in group undertakings.

In classrooms where the unit method had been introduced, teachers found a new freedom to help individual students with problems in the areas of reading, perhaps or arithmetic or English. Success in such areas was no longer measured by the progress of others but by the amount of progress the individual was making in terms of his capacity to learn in such areas. Therefore feelings of success were possible for the child no matter whether his activities served the group of which he was a member or whether he achieved progress in his own skill program. Teacher encouraged pupils to set their own goals in skill development and to judge their own success under guidance. Thus children often knew when they had succeeded and needed no mark or verification by the teacher. The democratic values involved were significant: the authority for what constituted success passed from the teacher to the pupil to a great extent, with accompanying feelings of self-respect, feeling of independence, and feeling of responsibility.

Numerous case studies were made on children with usual problems or experiences. One 11-year -old Bill, was known as a behaviour problem. He received from teachers and pupils alike more credit for mischief than was his duke because of his unfortunate reputation. He had lost all interest in school, preferring to play alone, his mother testified, in the fields or along the stream on his father's farm. When Bill entered Grade 5, the teacher, seeking to use some of her new-found knowledge gained in the cooperative curriculum study, capitalized upon the children's summer vacation experiences to initiate the unit: "How the United States Preserves. Its Beauty and Provides for Recreation." She helped Bill find a place on the committee and kept her eye on him during the organization and planning.

She suggested that the committee make use of Bill's special ability to find interesting things in the fields for exhibition in the class. All eyes turned on Bill with a new interest. Bill responded with an affirmative attitude; this was something he knew he could do. The next day he appeared in class with a large stone containing several unusual colours which he had found in the stream bed on the farm. The other children were gentlemanly appreciative, and Bill was definitely "in" with them. He promised to bring in other objects for the committee's exhibit and subsequently did.

Having tasted approval and success in one operation, the status and success-served boy tried his luck in other types of endeavour. He undertook to write the story of how he had discovered the large stone and how he had carried it to the house and later to school. Under the guidance of the teacher, he weighted the stone, compared it with various rock samples in the high school science laboratory, and found its properties and uses. He found a dictionary useful in finding the new words he needed to draft his story as well as to spell those he had heard about or previously used. Since the stone was composed of several metallic substances, the teacher suggested he compare its weight with other rocks or substances of comparable size. This suggestion set off a number or problem-solving activities in arithmetic which captured the notice and the participation of the entire class.

Bill submitted his draft of the story to the teacher for criticism before allowing committee members to see it. It was *his* story, but he wanted all the help he could get to make it good. After using some of the teacher's suggestions and correcting the mistakes in grammar and punctuation checked by her, Bill enlisted the help of his committee members also and finally became satisfied after rewriting the paper three times. The committee was glad to have Bill read the story to the class as a part of its progress report one Friday. He was proud but scared and yet he succeeded because he discovered everyone seemed to be on his side. The teacher obviously was proud of her own professional efforts, testifying that Bill was no longer a problem child but a new and inspired leader of his group.

There were many more cases—all success stories for both children and teachers. Who can gauge the lasting benefits of these acts of human conservation? Each case described contributed to the fulfilment of the major purposes of the curriculum which the Delta County group had resolved to provide for the children in its schools. There were indications that status, mastery, new experience, emotional security, functional skill development, and the rest were being built in a new curriculum rapidly coming to focus on mental hygiene.

The Diagnostic and Evaluation Program

Although each of the school involved in the study had been utilizing achievement batteries for diagnostic purposes, none had instituted a program supplementing these batteries with intelligence profiles, sociograms, mental health test, interest inventories, and other recent, useful instruments and techniques. The sociogram was used from the beginning of the study, and case studies developed during the second year. The full diagnostic program did not get into full swing in all schools until the third year. Change in marking and reporting progress was delayed deliberately until the communities became adjusted to the earlier changes in classroom method. However, this change had been completed in the elementary schools by the end of the third year and had received the enthusiastic approval of at lest on school board and the Parent - Teacher association of the same community.

The evaluation program moved away from mass achievement examinations for determining marks and the unfair competition attending them. Progress of the individual against his own record and in terms of his potential took the centre of interest. Teachers encouraged pupils to develop processes of self-evaluation. They helped each child maintain can individual folder which contained four sections: (1) a statement of the goals set by the committee in which he would be working and a record of achievements toward these goals; (2) a statement of the pupil's own current goals with a record of achievements; (3) samples of work done during the current unit or skills program; and (4) written appraisals by the student, the parent, and the teacher concerning the progress and the quality or work done by the pupil at weekly intervals or at the culmination of a unit of work. For each child the teacher kept folder containing intelligence profiles, achievement profiles, anecdotal records or case studies, health records, and other tests of instruments used for diagnostic purposes.

The pupil's folder could be taken home continually for perual by parents, and thus became the principal reporting medium. Regular conferences between teacher and parents became a part of the reporting procedure. The folder maintained by the teacher was used occasionally in teacher-parents reporting conference. The pupil's role in such conferences was to account for his own progress rather than to receive corrective directions. A more confidential report was given the parent after the dismissal of the pupil from the conference. Teachers reported that this procedure was very time-consuming but nevertheless very rewarding. Pupils assumed more responsibility for their learning and appeared to receive motivation from the reporting conferences. Where this method was tried, parents were enthusiastic in their praise for the procedure.

Implication of the New Curriculum

The teaching supervisory, and administrative staffs of the rural school of Delta County had placed emphasis upon curriculum change during the three years, and in so doing, might have misled some to assume that swift and unreasoning changes had taken place and that too little respect had been demonstrated for traditional educational practice. Important changes did take place in some of the schools enriching rather than displacing the time-honoured values. On the other hand, because of the blight of tradition there were unobserved opportunities to make worthwhile changes for the welfare of children. Few of the people involved in the project desired to have their program labelled "progressive." Rather, they desired to think that what they were doing was bases on sound research and experience, and while it was new to them in some respects, it was not new to other members of the teaching profession elsewhere. Their program, of course, has some unique characteristics, especially ask the new curriculum takes notice of local colour and resources. In general, the mental hygiene curriculum in Delta County is time-tested and calculated to develop better American citizens through a more truly American education. Finally, the program has as its central aim the development of psychological maturity among the children and youth who will spend their formative years in its educational climate.

SUMMARY

The imperative need of curriculum change to reduce the cultural lag manifest in education today should not need argumentation in order to elicit cooperative participation by all professional personnel in efforts to change the curriculum. This task will require the greatest possible efficiency and harmony if the professional community is to move toward the recognized goals of American education. These goals include the attitudes and behaviours of democracy. It is important to attack cooperatively indifference, pettiness, egocentricity, resentment, and intolerance. There is need to build among school people greater interest and enthusiasm for democratic participation in both professional and community affairs, to furnish situations which demonstrate that each person has a contribution to make to group endeavor, and to foster the disposition among teachers to share ideas for the best solution of common problem.

Since democracy depends for its existence upon effective group thinking, it is high time that professional school people develop true skill in the use of democratic process by utilizing and sharpening such skills constantly in all of their relationships. The degree of skill developed will determine ultimately the degree of success the society will achieve in making democracy operational in the general population.

Action research is the most promising process in any effort to improve the curriculum. It involves the participation of the people whose behaviour change is required if school operations are to be changed. There is an exploratory quality to action research which takes individual and groups to goals beyond their original expectations. Many people in America are aware of the need for curriculum change to meet the demands of life in the space age and especially to help humanity to grow up psychologically and socially, if not spirituality. This awareness must be translated into experimentation of the type provided by action research. Formal experimentation has its place in educational research; however, it has limited applicability to behavioural changes in teachers, parents, pupils, and administrators in the typical school situation. Action research changes people, and that is ultimately the only change that matters.

SELECTED READINGS

Amer, M. Benedict, "Helping Beginning Teacher, " *Bases for Effective Learning,* Thirty-first Yearbook , Washington, D.C. *The National Elementary Principal,* NEA, 1952. pp. 144-146.

Bailard, Virginia, "Teachers' Mental Health," *Clearing House,* XXVIII (January,1954); 283-284.

Burton, William H., and Brueckner, Leo J., *Supervision: A Social Process, 3rd* ed., New York, Appleton-Century-Crofts, Inc., 1955. Chapters 2-7, 12, and 16.

Dayton, Benjamin, "How Elementary Principals Can Improve Instruction," *American School Board Journal, CXXXII* (May, 1956), 37-39.

Drummond, Harold D., "Creating Good Living Conditions for Teachers, " *Bases for Effective Learning.* Thirty-first Yearbook, The National Elementary Principal, NEA, 1952, pp. 139-142.

"First-Year Teachers in 1954-5, " *National Education Association Research Bulletin,* XXXIV, No. 1 (February, 1956), 1-48.

Haake, Bernard, "A Letter to an Administrator," *Clearing House,* XXVIII (January, 1954) , 520-522.

Krug, Edward A., Babcock, Chester D., Fowlkes, John Guy, and James H. T. *Administering Curriculum Panning,* New York. Harper & Bros., 1956.

Entire book.

Krug, Edward A., *Curriculum Planning,* New York, Harper & Bros., 1957.

Entire book.

Linder, I. H. "Secondary principal and staff Morale," *American School Board Journal,* CXXXI (October, 1955), 25-27.

Otto, Henry, J., *Principles of Elementary Education,* rev, ed, New York, Rinehart and Co., 1955.

Chapters 9 and 15.

Shuster, Albert H., and Wetzler Wilson F., *Leadership in Elementary.*

REFERENCES

1. Stephen M. Corey, "Cooperative curriculum," *The Educational Courier,* XXV (December, 1954), 10.
2. Edward A. Krug, *et al. Administering Curriculum Planning,* New York, Harper & Bros, 1956, pp. 8-9.
3. Virgil E. Herrick, "Evaluating Curriculum Improvement Programs," *Educational Leadership,* VIII. No. 4 (January, 1951), 234.
4. Kenneth D. Benne and Muntyan Bazidar, *Human Relations in Curriculum Change,* New York, Dryden Press, Inc., 1951, pp. 66-96.
5. Herbert A. Thelen, "Group Dynamics in Curriculum Improvement," *Educational Leadership,* XI, No. 7 (April, 1954), 413-414.
6 J. W. Bushong, "Targets for the Young Administrator," *American School Board Journal* CXXXII (February, 1956), 29.
7. A. B. Hebeisen, "Look at Employee Morale," *Education,* November, 1955, p. 267.
8. This section, part of a monograph by W Ray Rucker, "A curriculum Focuses in Mental Health," was published by the Hogg Foundation for mental Hygiene, University of Texas, 1956, Reprinted with permission.
9. Kurt Lewin, Ronald Lippitt, and R.K. White, "Patterns of Aggressive Behavior in Experimentally Created "Social Climates," *Journal of Social*

Psychology, 10 (May, 1939), 271-299. See also Kurt Lewin, "Experiments in Autocratic and Democratic Atmospheres," *The Social Frontier* 4 (July, 1938), 316-319.

10. E. F. Lindquist (ed.), *Educational measurement,* Washington, D.C. American Council on Education, 1951, pp, 9-14. See also Willard C. Olson, "Redefining the Tasks of Education," *Educational Leadership,* IX (January, 1952), 222.

5

CURRICULUM IMPROVEMENT THROUGH SELF-EVALUATION

Cooperative self-evaluation of a school program by its own staff leads directly to curriculum improvement — improvement of teaching and learning— in such a way as to build teacher morale, develop wholesome democratic attitudes among members of the staff, and promote sustained professional growth by each individual teacher.

Sharing of ideas, techniques, growth by each teacher is one of the strengths of the profession and leads to professional growth by all. The process of sharing is especially helpful to those just beginning to teach. Modern instructional supervision seeks to stimulate sharing in very way possible.

Teachers constantly seek to improve the quality of teaching and learning in their classrooms. This is particularly true when they see a need for improvement, when they are given freedom to try their own ides, and when they are assisted by persons and processes.[1] The process of cooperative self-evaluation provides all of these conditions. Motivation is largely internal. Intrinsic to the process.

As an aid curriculum improvement, self-evolution takes teacher where they are, individually and as a group. It helps them to grow without feeling that they are being inspected or criticized. Thinking and planning are stimulated by group participation. Fears are reduced and feelings of security and status develop in the peer group. The focus is upon what is good for the children.

WHAT IS SELF- EVALUATION?

Self- evaluation of a school program implies an internal appraisal within a school or school system by those who are directly involved in the development of the curriculum. Individual on the professional staff, a committee of teachers in a grade level, vertical groups representing several levels or the entire school—all, depending upon the frame of reference, develop *appraisals of their practices by themselves*. Self-evaluation is the democratic process applied to program evaluation. This plan of self-appraisal is opposed to authoritarian appraisal by outsiders. It does not rule out help from the outside, but it encourages school or school system to take candid look at itself. Self-evaluation, then, implies mass involvement in evaluation by those who participate in what is to be evaluated.

Cooperative self-evolution of the school program is itself a process for professional growth. It leads to curriculum improvement. Emphasis is placed upon sharing the good helping the weak, developing staff morale and mental health, and developing an understanding by each individual of the total program of the school. It helps a school staff to develop the data and the self-assurance to meet hostile attacks on the school furnishes to the administrator, the school board, and the public a comprehensive report on the status of the school program together with plans for initiating improvements. Its focus is not upon individual teacher rating but upon the program of school life.

HOW SELF-EVALUATION WORKS

The plan for program evaluation presented in this chapter is suggested because of its workability, simplicity, and flexibility. The program can be undertaken and completed for report within a school year. Ideally this process will be undertaken by the staff each school year and become continuous program. It can be developmental, too, in that the tasks begun in one year may be continued in succeeding years. However, each year will have its comprehensive report which may be considered a progress report for programs extending for several years.

Before the plan can swing into operation, the school administrator should procure adequate copies of the criteria for distribution to staff members. The school board should be informed. The entire staff and school board should be given some orientation on the purposes and operation of the project. Provision should be made either for the appointment of committees or for the group to develop its own organization. Whether the committee chairmen, for instance, are to be appointed by administration or elected by the personnel of the particular committee involved may by a matter to be worked out during the orientation period. Individual teachers should be worked out during the their own written evaluation will not be identified by, or referred to, those above the grade level committee.

The operational process begins with the teacher who writes down *what he actually does in his teaching situation* in terms or the general evaluative criteria set forth below. The emphasis is upon recording what the teacher does in behavioural statements. Next, the descriptions of practices should be followed by a listings and analysis of strengths and weaknesses in these practices. The third step calls for a listings of suggested improvements with some suggestion on how these are to be carried out. Thus for each category under the general criteria, the evaluator will write: (1) description of practices, (2) an analysis or strengths and weaknesses, and (3) suggestions for improvement. This same pattern will be carried out in the reports of all individuals and committees including the final comprehensive report for the school as a whole.

The operational spotlight moves from the individual evaluations to the horizontal or grade level committee. Here the individual shares his practices, analyses, and suggestions with colleagues who teach on the same level. In this sharing process, teachers often boost the morale of their colleagues by observing that many good practices may have been recorded too modestly or some not at all. Participants will be alert to new ideas. The sharing of analyses of strengths and weaknesses as well as suggestions for improment can be every rewarding for the individual. It is a reach learning experience for all. This sharing of ideas in this horizontal committee can be one of the most important functions of the self-evaluation. The best ideas of this grouping will tend to become operation in all classrooms of the grade while the less desirable practices will tend to wither way. The report of the horizontal committee is a consensus or composite report in which the identity of the individual is lost. It is now a picture of the teaching program of that particular grade expressed in practices, strengths and weaknesses, and suggestions for improvement.

From the grade level committee, the program evaluation turns into the vertical stream. Several grade levels are grouped for a continuation of the sharing and analysing process begun in the horizontal committee. Thus, there may be a primary grade committee, and intermediate grade committee, etc., each eventually preparing a report of practices characteristic of the division. Each school or school system will decide how these divisional vertical groups should be organized on the basis of its size and other factors peculiar to its internal organization. Questions of sequence and articulation may enter the deliberations of these vertical committees. As before, the composite reports of these groups will be expressed in terms of practices, strengths and weaknesses, and suggestions for improvement.

The reports of the various divisional levels are received by a central committee of the school which is composed of representatives of each grade level (usually the chairman of the horizontal committee), representatives of parent or community groups, and representatives of supervision administration and the school board. This report becomes the summary report for the school as a whole. All problems affecting a total school program should be included in the deliberations even if not previously recorded in the reports submitted to the central committee.

If it is desirable to formulate a self-evaluation report for an entire school system, each school unit will undertake a program along the lines indicated above. Except in the case of large school districts, the reports of each school will be forwarded to a central committee of the school district composed of representatives of each school, representatives of parent groups, representatives of the school board, and representatives of the central administration and supervision staffs. The report of this committee will be forwarded to the superintendent and to the president of the school board.

For very large districts in large metropolitan areas, for instance, and additional horizontal grouping should be inserted into the above pattern for district-wide evaluation. Since composite reports will tend to disguise significant differences among schools, especially those with widely different socio-economic settings, schools, with similar community backgrounds should be grouped together for sharing and reporting. The characteristics of these differing community backgrounds and their inevitable effects on the curricula of the schools should be carefully noted in the final summary report for the school system.

At every level of the evaluative process, the free flow of ideas should stimulate both immediate and future improvements in the curriculum. A plan for continuous self-evaluation by the instructional staff should furnish a springboard for continuous curriculum development and professional growth.

THE USE EVALUATIVE CRITERIA

The criteria presented below do not structure evaluations to the point where practice is judged good or bad. Specific educational values will be discussed by each local group. Growth will take place in terms of where the group is at moment. Comparisons with teaching elsewhere are not necessarily intended. The general framework of the criteria has been developed with a view to the needs and characteristics of children, advancing educational thought, and the role of the school in a rapidly changing culture, but response to these criteria will guarantee no one correct answer. Each evaluation will necessarily be relative and unique. The criteria provide freedom for the individual and for the group to report the uniqueness of each situation by those who are closed to it.

6

ORGANISING A PROFESSIONAL DEVELOPMENT DAY

Many coordinators are concerned that they have had little training in running INSET events. There is no doubt that such an event can significantly affect the coordinator's influence within the school. It is therefore important to do the job properly. What follows is advice gleaned over a number of years from organising INSET events and assisting others to do so.

Common sense tells us that six hours of your colleagues' time is expensive. The knowledge can make organising an event intimidating even for the most experienced staff member. Schools and staff often have their own ideas as to when INSET days should take place. Whilst there is no ideal time of the year, it is worth considering the advantages of meeting towards the end of a break or in the early stages of a term when teachers are refreshed.

The following points, whilst not ensuring success, will mean that progress is more likely.

Step 1 — Clearly the Purpose of the Day

If possible begin planning in the terms prior to the event. Consider your experience of previous events; what did you learn? Will you set the day within a theme such as planning or assessment? Can you build on previous events? What precisely do you think the school and your colleagues need to get out of the day?

Canvass colleagues' opinions, and seek advice from the deputy and headteacher for detailed guidance. If you are apprehensive, try to be clear about what you believe is needed. Prepare and circulate a simple proposal for the day. This will allow everyone to give you feedback. Make sure that you listen. Remember that colleagues have other priorities and they under considerable pressure. Part of your aim is to reassure, so be sensitive to your colleagues and their needs.

Establish an aim, try to written this in a sentence or two. Read as widely as possible so that you are up to date.

Step 2 — Begin io Plan

Now that you are more clear about the day you can start to think about the nature of the activities.

You might include:

- an ice breaking activity;
- an introduction (including a statement of aims);
- practical activity;
- brainstorming;
- groupwork;
- snowballing;
- plenary session at the end oi each main block of time;
- recaps as you move onto new areas;
- flexibility (time and content);
- visits to part of the school (a resource base) or further afield;
- time to consider classroom management (this is often a key issue);
- well prepared resources (you may need to borrow items, beware of replying on other people);
- an outside (advisory teacher, teacher, advisor, college or university lecturer);
- alternate practical and talking sessions;
- collaboration with another school (advantages and disadvantages);
- the needs of teachers of early years and those who work with older children;

— evaluation;

— a conclusion.

Formulate an outline plan for the day, keep your aim firmly in mind and beware of being over optimistic about thing! It is often a good idea to include coffee breaks within period of practical work.

Remember that teachers do need a break. It is better to work hard for a short period than prolong the activities.

Always plan to summarise and recap after a break. Say what you think you have achieved so far and what you intend to do next.

Step 3 — Plan the Detail

Revise your plans in greater detail. Something may well go wrong on the day which cannot be avoided. Do not add to that possibility through lack of care.

Make sure that:

— everyone knows the arrangements, including part-time and temporary staff;

— non-teaching staff are aware of what is happening;

— any printing is done in advance, with extra copies of everything;

— the room will be large enough, the right temperature and comfortable (small chairs can cause great discomfort!);

— any documents required will be available;

— stationery is on hand;

— videos and computers work — check them the previous day and again immediately before you start;

— lunch arrangements are made and agreed.

Set the tone:

— show that you are interested in how colleagues feel;

— if you are young, beware that you may appear to be a great threat to colleagues who have taught for many years, so be seen to take advice;

— prepare everything prior to the event. You may be able to

negotiate some time for this, but do not expect it;

— where possible and relevant do related work with your children prior to the event; don't ask people to do what you have not done or are not prepared to do;

— it may be worth circulating an article, notes or a prompt sheet prior to the event.

Step 4 — Running the Day

If you are well prepared you will not be dashing around five minutes before you start. This is a useful time to chat and gauge the mood of the group. To start with, go through an outline of the day and emphasis the flexibility you have included. Clearly state at the beginning what you hope go get out of the day. Also state the limitations of the day. Talk briefly about the evaluation of the day. Emphasises that you aim to have a product at the end of the day and state what its nature is likely to be and how you will get there. Try to move to some sort of simple ice-breaking activity fairly quickly, such as:

> 'I'd like you to spend five minutes listing all the play activities which go on in your room. I will then ask one or two people to read out part of their list.'

Participate yourself throughout the day, moving between groups. Don't allow anyone to dominate discussion — a very effective blocking strategy often used by politicians! Rehearse your tactics for moving the discussion on. Have a number of supplementary questions which you will use if required. Try to avoid being didactic. Be prepared to summarise DFE, SCAA and LEA documents. During small group discussions take two minutes to check your plans and have the next step at your fingertips.

Don't reply on technology, videos etc. Used carefully they can help enormously, but can they easily be overused and can break down. Avoid long periods of talk in the afternoon, especially the 'graveyard' slot immediately after lunch. Try to relax and enjoy yourself. You will have worked hard for this day and some parts can be expected to go better than others. Try to work towards clear statements of intent, so that everyone is certain about the action that will be required. It may be useful to finish off with the formulation of an action plan, where you will need to begin to delegate tasks. Identify a longer period of time (one term, one year) after which you will review any developments following the event.

Do plan time for evaluation either at the end of every session or at the end of the day, focusing on the positive and the negative aspects of the day.

- What did you get out of this activity?
- To what extent will you be to implement this in your classroom? What are the constraints?
- How did you feel about the day, its pacing, timing and content?
- Did you get sufficient opportunity to offer your own ideas?
- Are you clear about the next step?
- How would you like to follow up this activity?

This information will be very valuable to you as you plan and negotiate for resources, and time in the future. Do not take criticism personally, it will help you to improve your future INSET days.

Step 5 — Taking Stock

Collate the evaluation of the day and note down your impressions. Make a short summary of the main outcomes of the day. Colleagues will quickly forget their words and any promises they might have made.

Negotiate a review with the headteacher or the deputy so that you can clearly outcomes and determine the best way forward which will fit in with the school's overall direction.

Professional development days can create an enormous momentum in the school. These events always need following up. They are never an end in themselves. Time is a precious commodity so it is essential that the day is viewed as a success and that there is a positive outcome with realistic, achievable targets, such as:

- a new resource
- a document
- an organisational system
- a parents' meeting.

This will help everyone to feel that their time on the day did lead to something, and it will make it easier when you want to repeat the process. The best way to facilitate change is to provide for positive experiences.

BIBLIOGRAPHY

Eason, P. *Making School Centred INSET Work,* OU Press, London, 1985.

Leyland, G. Taking the Pain Out of Training, *Questions,* pp 16, 17 December 1988.

7
THE HISTORY IN THE CURRICULUM

INTRODUCTION

The question 'National Curriculum History — how will get it all in?' is most frequently herd when teachers discuss the history Programmes of Study. Following closely are questions concerning the methodology, the resourcing and the assessment of history in the primary school. These questions are perfectly understandable when you look at the record of history teaching in primary education. As most coordinators realise, history has been, and probably still is, the least taught subject in the primary school. HMI surveys of 1978 and 1989 found little evidence of it, and where it *was* being taught, they judged it to be less than adequate in 80% of infant classes and 66% of junior classes seen. This probably means that you, as the history coordinator, will be working with many people who may never have considered history as an essential ingredient in their curriculum provision, but rather as a 'bolted on' fragment to another topic.

The National Curriculum now makes history teaching mandatory on a profession which has had little experience of teaching it and with meagre resources. You will need to develop in teachers both an understanding of the nature of history and a pedagogy to sustain quality history teaching and learning in the primary school.

This means spending time with staff discussing fundamental questions, such as:

— Is it true that history was not taught in your school?

— Why should it be taught?

— What should be taught?

— How should it be taught?

If we look at these questions again we might tease out some possible replies. Eventually you will have to go through the process with staff yourself, because it is counter-productive to pre-empt their discussion with your own guesses.

Why Was History Not Taught?

The variety of answers you receive will show the background and professional experiences of the teachers you work with. The replies will also alert you to their views of how children learn. Some teachers will maintain that history was taught to them, often at secondary school, as chalk and talk description of the past, which they then had to and reproduce for an exam. This was not and experience they would want to repeat with primary children. Others will no doubt argue that young children's historical thinking is severely limited by their stages of cognitive development and that history should be left until they are older. Yet others will say that unless young children can be engaged in active, first-hand learning experiences, they will not retain much of what they are taught. These colleague' resistance to history will be built on the same premier as the first group I mentioned — namely that history is a transferable package of greed knowledge from teacher to taught.

All these different perceptions will need to be thoroughly discussed with staff in the light of your understanding of history as a process of interpretation as well as a knowledge of facts.

Why should it be taught?

A strong sense of why history is being taught should pervade all curriculum planning, influencing the selection of content and methods of teaching.

1.4 History Non-Statutory Guidance

The simple answer to this question is - because it is a statutory requirement. However, you will only get vigorous worthwhile teaching from teachers who believe that what they are teaching is right for their children's all-round development. The vast majority of teachers in primary schools, who have not taught history in any focused sense before, will feel vulnerable and guarded when confronted with the National

Curriculum history requirements because these call into question their previous teaching emphases.

If you acknowledge this and proceed carefully as you work to enthuse your colleagues about the history curriculum then you are more likely to gain some success and see them begin to develop as effective teachers of history to young children.

Encouraging teachers to acknowledge that history has an important place in the primary curriculum will make your job, of enhancing their skills and confidence to do it, considerably easier. Philosophy has a bad press lately with its place in teacher education derided as of no practical value. Thinking about such fundamentals such as 'Why teach history?' is a most useful exercise if it clarifies ideas and opinions. It will affect practice quite radically.

As history coordinator you need to make the time to discuss the purposes of school history with your colleagues. You could use those listed in the Non-Statutory guidance as a start. It is always helpful to begin with the teacher's own views, however, before producing the 'official line'. The purposes of school history are listed as follows in the Non-Statutory Guidance:

> There are two main aims of school history:
>
> — to help pupils develop a sense of identity through learning about the development of Britain, Europe and the world;
>
> — to introduce pupils to what is involved in understanding and interpreting the past.
>
> Other purposes follow:
>
> — to arouse interest in the past;
>
> — to contribute to pupils' knowledge and understanding of other countries and cultures;
>
> — to understand the present in the light of the past;
>
> — to enrich other areas of the curriculum;
>
> — to train the mind by disciplined study;
>
> — to prepare pupils for adult life.

Each purpose is worth discussing with your staff. If this is done, the purposes will not remain theoretical statements of good intent, but become translated into achievable objectives with classes of children specifically in mind. Think about the first aim as an example:

How can you, as coordinator, help children develop a sense of identity through learning about Britain, Europe and the World?

Does it feed your children's sense of identity to be told about the Vikings, Greeks, Maya, Victorians or Tudors? Of course not. This can only be achieved by finding effective links between the children's experience now with that of people in the past. In this way you will nurture their sense of identity. By engaging in these sorts of discussions, teachers will see that the simple transmission of history facts is not what the primary history teacher is about.

What should be Taught?

This may seem an unnecessary question at first glance because, after all, the content of the content of the history curriculum is laid out in the Programme of Study as Study Units. However, two very important points need to be made:

1. The history curriculum was designed by a group of people who had never taught in primary schools although one primary teacher was brought on to the Committee at a late stage. We all have ideas about the relative importance of various periods in history and it is useful to debate this to increase out historical awareness. I believe it will be more beneficial for the development of history teaching if you encourage teachers to regard the content of the National Curriculum as a first attempt at providing a curriculum for the primary child, rather than to accept it as if 'carved in tablets of stone'.
2. This point grows out of the first. Many primary teachers believe the amount of history children are expected to cover is totally unrealistic given the demands of the rest of the National Curriculum plus the themes, skills and dimensions. This means teachers will have to select *within* the Study Units. You will be involved in deciding which aspects of the content should be given more emphasis and therefore more time at the expense of other aspects.

INSET ACTIVITIES

It will be useful to carry out a couple of short INSET activities to alert teachers to the central importance of continued debate about 'what' history?

Who is important in history?

Put up a piece of string across the room. Ask teachers to write on slips of paper two or three names of people who lived in the past to whom they would like to talk and question. Then give them paper clips to attach these papers onto the string 'time-line' in chronological sequence. You should identify which end of string is the present and which one in the distant past.

This exercise nearly always illustrates the glaring omissions in the history teaching experienced by the participants as children. Historical men predominate, with the inevitable addition of Florence Nightingale and Boadiceea. Children are never mentioned. History is portrayed, when viewed from these lines, as the story of rich, powerful men in Britain of Europe. When this exercise has been completed, look again at the purposes of school history, one of which is to help pupils develop a sense of identity.

Discuss with teachers whether their feelings of identity are heightened or marginalised by looking at the lines. In other words, 'What does history say about me if I am a Welsh, working class woman?'

The statements game

Teachers will have many ideas about the nature of history. These may be explored by statements used to provoke debate, such as:

— History is a series of events to be learned in chronological order.

— History is about enquiry into the past, identifying, interpreting and selecting evidence which appears to be relevant.

— History tells us how modern man is superior to the cave man.

— History is concerned with understanding, seeing the past from the inside, from another's position, empathetically.

- History is concerned not with conveying accepted facts but with making informed judgements, and displaying of the evidence on which those judgements are made.
- History can introduce children to some understanding of what is meant by 'true' in human affairs.

Ask colleagues singly and later in pairs to make up their own definitions of history to add to this list. In general discussion, these can be sorted, prioritised or discarded.

Activities such as these will help teachers grow in their understanding of history as the complex subject it is.

How Should History be Taught?

Content or process?

This question can only be answered when you, as history coordinator, are clear in your mind as to what history is. History is two things: the past, and the study of the past. If you believe the past is an agreed, unchangeable body of knowledge then you will study in a different way than if you consider history to be constantly in need of reinterpretation. Again, discussion with colleagues is important to clarify how history should be taught. History as 'process' involves an examination of sources and making interpretations in a critical appraising way, in order to generate theories about their validity and reliability. In other words history methodology is characterised by scrupulous respect for evidence and disciplined use of the imagination. Encouraging teachers to view children as budding historians will certainly help to channel their energies.

The history biased topic

While there seems to be a move towards subject specific teaching at Key Stage 2, it is unlikely to be the answer as to now to fit the content of the nine subject areas into the time available. The way forward seems to be for focused and carefully planned **subject biased** topic work. Your job will be to give history the highest possible profile when its turn comes for special attention.

The teacher's role

You need to work with staff so that they use their discussion and questioning time effectively with children. Teachers are supremely able at developing oral language through discussion, but they need to encourage children's historical skills and concepts and to develop a critical approach to historical evidence. For example, children may be looking at building and noting such things as the number and type of windows, the materials used in its construction and counting the people using it. This is fine as an information gathering exercise. To help the children to think historically, however, the teacher has to get them to ask such questions as:

- how old is the building **(Time)**;
- has it changed in any way since it was built **(Continuity / change)**;
- why gave the changes occurred **(Cause / Consequence)** ;
- can you put the changes in chronological order **(Sequence)**;
- is the building like the others near it **(Similarity / Difference)**;
- why has it survived;
- what evidence have you to support your conclusions;
- is the evidence sufficient?

Whole school planning: the history curriculum

If teachers have gone through some of the processes outlined above with you, the job of developing a whole-school approach to the history curriculum will be very much easier. They will be more confident about the particular contribution history has to make to children's cognitive and affective development. In addition, then views of what history is to them will clarify other aims and objective for teaching primary history. They will still be somewhat overawed, in all probability, by the volume of the Programmes of Study and feel insecure about their own subject knowledge as a basis for teaching many Study Units. They may therefore need support to see the value of whole-school planning. Some key points about the necessity of a whole-school plan are outlined below.

Why whole-school planning?

To ensure:

- — continuity within and between Key Stage 1 and Key Stage 2;
- — progression in content, concepts, skills and attitudes from Year 1 to Year 6;
- — balance between the various types of history: social; political, cultural and aesthetic religious, economic, technological and scientific;
- — balance between local, national and world history;
- — balance between ancient and modern history;
- — balance between the history of men; women and children, rich and poor, powerful and powerless.

In addition:

- — to decide the timing of the core units at Key Stage 2;
- — to priorities the collection of resource to support these decisions;
- — to highlight aspects of INSET provision as essential if the school is to move forward in its history provision.

Agreement about all these aspects is vital, so that the child moving through the primary school has the opportunity of sampling the richness and variety of history.

Alongside this preoccupation with whole-school planning should run another important consideration. This should be regarded as an INSET activity for you to used with the staff to develop their history teaching skills.

Interpretation of the statements of attainment

The Attainment Targets provide the concepts and skills particular to history in the form of statements of attainment. These are supposed to be hierarchically descriptive criteria of children's growing historical understanding. Whether they are or not will become clear as teachers and children use them and make judgements about their appropriateness. For the present, it seems essential that teachers should develop their own understanding of these historical concepts and skills and consider how they might incorporate them into their teaching. You, as history coordinator, have a central role in drawing the attention of staff to this need through providing curriculum development time.

Planning the history curriculum

While most of the history curriculum is set out in the Core Study Units there are still some choices to be made from the **supplementary units** and these need to be carefully considered.

Obviously, having and expert on the staff on the Indus Valley or Mesopotamia would influence your choice, but given that in the typical school no-one will profess to know anything about any of the supplementary units in Section C (Ancient Egypt, Mesopotamia, Assyria, The Indus Valley, The Maya, Benin) which should your colleagues select?

Consideration needs to centre on the Programme of Study and how its assessment will be handled.

Whichever unit is chosen there must be opportunities for children to behave like historians: to handle evidence, draw tentative conclusions about it and understand how there may be different interpretations of what they are studying. If they only have access to textbook based evidence, them that may be one reason for not choosing that particular period to study.

The unit based on **local history** (Section B) is very much more complex than the local environment study that was so common in primary practice in the past. First of all, there is a need to keep the **historical** nature of the study in focus, even though other areas of the curriculum, such as geography, art and design, and technology naturally occur. The prescriptive nature of the descriptors implies that you; as history coordinator, will need to do quite a bit of homework to find out as much as much as you can about the locality. Then you can begin to formulated what you know into manageable packages of information relevant to the staff and children as well as identifying sources which are accessible to the children.

The unit involving the study of a theme over a long period of time has to be chosen from a set whose titles look largely familiar. They are very general, like the titles of the all-embracing, loosely planned topic webs which were once acceptable. Choosing a unit which could supplement one of the Core Units would seem to be the ideal way of providing extra cohesion and progression to your history curriculum.

ASSESSMENT

History is unique among the subjects of the National Curriculum in having a totally integrated syllabus and assessment procedure. As the document says:

> 'The attainment targets and their constituent statements of attainment specify the knowledge, skills and understanding which pupils of different abilities and maturities are expected to have by the end of each Key Stage. The programmes of study specify the matters, skills and processes which are required to be taught to pupils. The two types of requirement are complementary and pupils will not be able to satisfy the statements of attainment without demonstrating a knowledge and understanding of the historical of the appropriate programme of study'.

Because the Programmes of Study describe the content and the attainment targets as conceptually based, there is no way they can remain divorced at the planning stage. You may need to remind your colleagues of this, so that while they are planning they will also be looking at how the outcomes can be assessed within the three attainment targets. While this may be difficult for staff to grasp initially, some joint planning sessions with you — either at the whole staff, Key Stage 1 and 2, or individual teacher level — should set them on them on the right path. One of the best ways develop staff assessment abilities is to discuss, at length if necessary, what the statements of attainment actually mean. Clarifying this area is essential, because the staff will them have a common definition in mind when they make their assessments of children's progress. For example:

AT 3:2 — 'recognise that historical sources can stimulate and help answer questions about the past'.

Differing interpretations of the word 'recognise' would lead to wide variations in the awarding of the statement. Encouraging staff to justify their understanding of the statements will lead to consensus through a moderating process. Once staff have become used to looking for assessment opportunities at the planning stage, they will realise the need for good quality resources which will help them in their teaching and assessment of children.

This brings us on to the next big area of preoccupation for the history coordinator: the resources needed to help implement the National Curriculum.

RESOURCES

As history was rarely taught in primary schools, it is not surprising that resources for it were meagre and consisted of an over-reliance on textbooks or TV programmes. However, the National Curriculum has emphasised the process side of history, you will remind your staff. This demands that children are allowed to learn about the past from a range of historical sources, inclucding artefacts, pictures and photographs, music, adults talking about their past, documents and printed source, building and sites and computer based material.

Two Problems Immediately Spring to Mind

1. Where do you get these sources from?

Remember that one of your main purposes in teaching history to young children is to give them a sense of personal identity. You will therefore need to look for sources within the community that the school serves. Artefacts — the correct term for manufactured objects looked at historically — are plentiful in every house and garden. Think of the change in domestic irons over the last fifteen year (even if you cannot get any older than that). Children will bring in pieces of clothing, books and toys, which can be handled in a historical way to discuss change and continuity, causation and time. Similarly, pictures and photographs are readily available. The older members of the community are treasure troves of memories and opinions so interview them about any of their experiences. The local built environment is near at hand, familiar yet interesting to budding historians. Written sources do not have to be marriage or birth certificates. They can be local newspaper accounts of famous local events or sporting stories, they can be postcards and letters from different periods, or the school log, old advertisements, recipe books or catalogues.

Start collections based on the community you serve, but also develop resources for the other study units. Indeed lack of material may lead you to choose something else to study or to look for another aspect within a study unit to concentrate upon. One of the reasons why Egyptians (from Section C in the Supplementary Units,) are very popular in Manchester is probably related to the superb permanent display of Egyptology at the University of Manchester Museum. You will no doubt find similar types of exhibitions in your area. It is of course useful to network with other history coordinationators in your area in order to build up a resource pack of places to visit.

Providing each Unit with source material can be an arduous undertaking. This is partly, though not exclusively, your job. Through staff discussion, there will be 'share out' of units according to age groups. Each teacher will need to research and make provision for their particular units. You have a role — not to do all the running around necessary to collect materials — but to support and direct teachers' energies towards fruitfully areas, where their enthusiasm and confidence can grow. Practically, of course, teachers will need time so that they can visit archives or sites in preparation for their planning.

History from the Victorians onwards is relatively easy to deal with in this manner, but how do you it for the Vikings or Tudors? If you can find no way of giving children access to first-hand investigative experiences, you will not be able to assess them on the attainment targets. Encourage teachers to give a brief talk about these phenomena and move on to more useful aspects. For example, the Vikings are only one aspect of the huge topic, 'Invaders and Settlers'. If your school is based near Roman or Anglo Saxon settlement remains, then it is sensible to focus work on these. Similarly, if you are close to Tudor buildings, then beginning a topic on these will lend point to your ultimate aim of discussing aspects of the Tudor Age.

2. What do you do with the resources when you have collected them?

In a sense you had specific aims in mind for your collections, so you and the staff will be committed to teaching and assessing history already, through first-hand experiences using primary or secondary sources, wherever possible. There is still a good deal of INSET to do to ensure that teachers use the resources in a historically accurate way to develop children's historical understanding. Too often, the activity can end up as a useful oral language session or an inspiring children's historical concepts. To keep a check on how resources are used and their effectiveness, it helps to clarify, through staff meetings, the purpose of any materials introduced into the classroom for the teaching and learning of history. I have listed the key types of materials with references for you to follow up on their uses in the classroom. It is essential to go through the process of understanding about the merits or demerits of particular resources with the staff, rather than giving them a list and telling them get on with it. (Remember the acrimony surrounding the introduction of the National Curriculum for the same reason.)

RESOURCES AND REFERENCES

This is a very brief and indicative section on resources, with what I consider are key publications where appropriate. I have made more notes on sections such as Written Sources and Equal Opportunities (page 48) and Multicultural Education (page 50), because I feel strongly about these. However, each section could be expanded into a chapter. You could profitably work on these headings, build up a resource file of how to use the various types of evidence and add references to materials and schemes which you find particularly helpful.

1. Artefacts, portraits and pictures

Morris, S. A. *Teacher's Guide to Using Portraits,* English Heritage, 1990.

Durbin, G., Morris, S., Wilkinson, S. *A Teacher's Guide to Learning from Objects,* English Heritage, 1990.

In addition, and useful for INSET purposes, English Heritage produce a Slide Pack 'Using Portraits' which takes you through twelve slides with careful notes so that your observation skills are enhanced.

2. Stories and Narrative

HMI. *History in the Primary and Secondary Years,* DES, 1985.

HMI. *Aspects of Primary Education. The Teaching and Learning of History and Geography,* DES, 1989.

Cox, Kath and Hughes, Pat. *Early Years History: An Approach Through Story,* Liverpool Institute of Higher Education, Stand Park Road, Liverpool, L 16 9JD.

Farmer, Alan. Story-Telling in History, *Teaching History,* January, 1990.

Little, Vivienne and John, Trevor. Historical Fiction in the Classroom, *Teaching of History Series No. 59,* The Historical

Association, 1988.

Sets of books are also available from:

Landley Madeline. *Early Years History: An Approach through Story.* 79 Acorn Centre, Barry Street, Oldham, OL1 3NE.

Stories for Time book box from Badger Publishing Limited, Unit One, Parsons Green Estate, Boulton Roadm, Stevenage. Herts, SG1 4QG.

3. Oral History

Purkis, Sallie. *Thanks for Memory,* Collins Educational, 1987.

4. Buildings

For further information on this primary source see the English Heritage series of videos and accompanying booklets for various historic sites. The English Heritage also produces a series for videos which show how a historian needs to be like a detective, looking for clues and evidence in order to reach conclusions about buildings and objects. These can be fruitfully discussed in staff development time. Information for these and all English Heritage material can be obtained from: English Heritage Education Service, Key Sign House, 429 Oxford Street London. W1R 2HD. Tel: 071 973 3442/3

5. Written Sources

There is a rich variety of documentary material available such as school log books, census returns, parish records, letters, inventories and government reports marriage and birth certificates and wills. In addition, newspapers, directories, advertisements, posters and other printed matter provide useful material on which to work.

Original documentation will probably be precious and available only to look at carefully and not to work from. Photocopies of these are good substitute for they provide children with a chance to study the layout, language and writing of the original without fear of damage. You should collect as wide a variety of these materials as possible, but it is essential to catalogue them to ensure that staff know their whereabouts and that they have decided how best they may be used.

One aspect of documentary evidence needs exploring with the staff. A piece of writing from Victorian times will be difficult for children to decipher, while a piece from the Tudor period will be almost impenetrable. Should this be copied into present day script and the language 'modernised'? The answer depends on what you want the children to get from it. **Essentially, the medium is as important as the message so should not be tampered with lightly.** The act of carefully looking at and deciphering text is an important and necessary skill for all historians — one children should be inducted into as soon as possible. The more they look at the text, the more easily they will be able to read it, especially in the company of an adult who can help them along when they get stuck. These factors need discussion between you and the staff, so that they begin to appreciate that reading documents that have been translated into modern script (and even into modern language) and answering questions on them is essentially just a comprehension exercise, like those they do in their English work.

Reference

One pack of documents which makes the past accessible to children has been produced by Charlotte Mason College and Cumbria Archive Service. It is called *Could do Better. Children at School 1870-1925.*

6. Living History

This involves children in a dramatic reconstruction of an event in the past. It is useful to inform staff of what is available within reasonable travelling distance in terms of 'In Role' Days so that these can be planned within a topic rather than become a 'bolt-on' afterthought. The costs involved make it essential that there is maximum followup, so that the children get the most out of the experience and Governors and parents also feel the money has been well spent.

7. Information Technology

Its first and most significant contribution to the history curriculum has in the databases that can be created to deal with the material generated from studies involving the local community such as census returns or school rolls.

The second area where IT can enhance the history curriculum is through the series of computer-aided learning programs. These are becoming readily available from publishers, but you must be discriminating in the choice of programs which will fully support good teaching.

8. TV and Published History Schemes

One important piece of information to disseminate regularly to staff until they absorb it, is that **HMI found that where was poor primary history practice there was also over-reliance on TV programmes and published schemes.** You will appreciate that a published history scheme, available for teachers who have rarely taught history, is a sort of security blanket. Even if is not used much, it is there for comfort and support. If you have worked carefully and effectively through the activities mentioned earlier teachers will come to their own realisation of what history is and how should be taught, and their desire for schemes will diminish rapidly. There is good material on the market, of course, but there is also a lot that is not suitable for teaching history as effectively as a resource bank built specifically to meet the needs of a particular set of children tackling a particular study unit.

EQUAL OPPORTUNITIES AND MULTICULTURAL EDUCATION

National Curriculum history requires that children are taught about the cultural and ethnic diversity of past societies and the experiences of men and women. Therefore each time a study unit is planned these two requirements should be carefully catered for. There are, however, several difficulties to which you must alert the staff:

1. We have all been exposed to history teaching supported by text books which have largely ignored the part played by women and minority ethnic groups in the development of our society. We must be aware of this bias in our own knowledge so that we do not pass it on by default to our children.
2. Even today many primary schools have history textbooks dating back several decades. Of course, it is tempting to keep them on the basis that anything is better than nothing! However, it is probable they will have negative or non-existent images of women and ethnic minorities in them. Two things can be done bout this. The books can be removed from the classrooms. This rids the children of these images. More imaginatively, the books can be used

to develop children's awareness of bias (AT2) and to develop their ability in the use of sources.(AT3).

3. Your school will no doubt have an equal opportunities and multicultural education set of guidelines. It is sensible to use the principles involved in setting up those as a basis for planning your history units.

REFERENCES

Collicott, Sylvia, *A Woman's Place in Junior Education,* May 1991. This is an excellent article to use as a basis for staff discussion as they are encouraged to explore their own understanding of women in history. The article also gives several references for materials on women's history.

Collicott, Sylvia. *Connections,* Haringey Local-National -World Links, 1986. Published by Haringey Community Information Service in association with the Multicultural Curriculum Support Group, Central Library, Wood Green, High Road, London, N22.

The title describes what the book is about. It illustrates that many races and cultures have been mixed into our society for hundreds of years. The book gives an extensive bibliography as well as suppliers' addresses for books for a multicultural society.

CONCLUSION

The history coordinator has more new ground to break in terms of developing staff expertise than perhaps any other subject coordinator except the IT coordinator. You will need to pace your input very carefully so as not to overface or panic your hard-pressed colleagues. The best way of developing staff confidence in teaching history is for you to pilot various methods and materials, share your findings before encouraging colleagues to share their own successes with the rest of the staff. Staff development exercises which involve looking at how to use a resource and also how to plan for progression is another way in which you can ensure children get a broadly balanced history curriculum. Ultimately, though, your personal enthusiasm for history will be a crucial factor in the staff's commitment to its place in the primary curriculum.

8

APPROACH TO PHYSICAL EDUCATION

A fundamental problem encountered by the PE coordinator is that many class teachers, and more significantly perhaps headteachers, do not understand the purpose of PE. They often regard it merely as an extension of playtime or an unnecessary interruption in the serious business of the school day. The unique organisational and teaching approaches are also seen as inhibiting factors. The prospect of a large group of children free from the relative constraints of the classroom can strike terror into the heart of even the most experienced teacher. Some teachers regard the hall and playground as alien environment to be avoided whenever possible. Preparations for any kind of festivity or even mildly inclement weather are readily seized upon as reasons for cancelling PE.

There are other reasons why PE may be unpopular with your teachers. Some have negative images of the subject arising from personal unhappy experiences, particularly at secondary school. The emphasis in teaching PE now however, and especially at the primary level, is on the involvement of all children and certainly not just those who have a natural aptitude for physical activity. Teachers must also have noticed that when children to have PE, everyone usually enjoys it enormously.

It is regrettable therefore that many teachers have only limited experience of teaching this subject. They are missing:

— the fun and satisfaction for teacher and pupil alike;

— the opportunities for establishing, improving and

maintaining good teacher-pupil relationships offered by an environment different from the classroom.

A major factor influencing primary school teachers' reluctance to reach PE must lie in the inadequate time spent on PE in Initial Teacher Training Courses. Surveys — including those by the Physical Education Association in 1987 and, in the case of dance, the Calouste Gulbenkian Foundation in 1989 — consistently confirm that courses are so brief that potential teachers are barely given a cursory acquaintance with any aspect of the subject. Indeed it is fairly common for some teachers to receive no training at all! All In-service Training in PE has rarely been regarded as a priority, it is hardly surprising that teachers feel so insecure.

There has been little incentive to data for individual teachers to improve their knowledge, skills and understanding of PE. Few will have been in a school where the headteacher was a PE enthusiast. Consequently, the implementation of a National Curriculum presents a daunting prospect to many. Schools are required to provide all children with experience in six PE activities;

- games
- gymnastics
- dance
- athletics
- swimming
- outdoor and adventurous activities.

Furthermore there are certain levels of attainment to take into account.

Who will help the class teacher to fulfil the statutory requirements of the National Curriculum and also to ensure continuity, progression and consistency through a whole-school approach? You the PE curriculum coordinator have this responsibility and it is likely to be a daunting prospect! No-one could be expected to began with an all-embracing knowledge, but there are certain key areas on which you should focus:

- Strengthen your expertise, concentrating initially on the three central activities of gymnastics, games and dance. Acquiring or deepening your knowledge and understanding should be a priority.

— Familiarise yourself with the National Curriculum End of Key Stage Statements, Programmes of Study and also Non-Statutory Guidance in PE at Key Stages 1 and 2.

— Learn what is involved in the assessment and recording of children's progress in PE.

— Make yourself thoroughly familiar with the full range of organisational strategies and teaching techniques for PE.

— Learn how to budget, care for and manage equipment and other resources.

You can acquire this knowledge and expertise in a variety of ways, such as attending INSET courses offered by LEAs and Institutes of Higher Education, and by personal efforts, such as the scrutiny of teaching handbooks and videotapes, visiting other school and so on. Other skills than those of a PE teacher are also necessary, however. In the first chapter it was stressed that the curriculum coordinator is essentially a manager. You will have to work alongside your colleagues persuading and cajoling them into accepting necessary change. You must therefore endeavour to increase their understanding and improve their practice. A number of useful suggestions were made in Chapter One.

This fundamental aspect of the role is underlined in the discussion paper by Robin Alexander, John Rose and Chris Woodhead *Curriculum and Practice in Primary Schools.* They suggest that although curriculum coordinators have developed expertise in the writing of syllabuses and the provision of resources, they have been less successful in the major task of influencing other teachers. How you can use a whole-school approach to systematically improve your colleagues' practice in teaching PE is the focus of this chapter.

An important means of influencing others is by personal enthusiasm which will grow with your increasing knowledge and understanding. An enthusiast arouses interest and curiosity; enthusiasm is catching; but enthusiasm is not enough. You also need to be persuasive and articulate in advocating PE as offering valuable experiences for children.

WHY IS PHYSICAL EDUCATION IMPORTANT?

What arguments can you employ to convince your colleagues that PE should be taken seriously? Teachers must be motivated in order to develop the necessary knowledge, organisational skills and teaching techniques. You will also need to present should arguments to your headteacher and governors when competing for resources.

In her chapter in the book by Tessa Roberts, *Encouraging Expression,* Patricia Sanderson argues the PE experiences make valuable contributions to the development of the whole child by offering integrated education of the physical, cognitive, personal and social, creative and aesthetic aspects. You may find some of these arguments helpful to use with your teachers.

Physical Development

It is a good idea to begin by stressing the importance of PE for physical development. Most teachers will agree that in today's sophisticated society, children are not getting enough exercise. They may also be aware of research at Exeter University which consistently reveals how unfit children of primary school age and the serious implications this can have for the development of the heart muscle, possibly contributing to heart disease in later life. Regular exercise is essential for the normal growth of other muscle tissue as well as bones. You could remind colleagues that without PE in school, some children would get virtually no exercise. Of course PE lessons must be vigorous if they are to make any impact on a child's level of fitness. This is something you will need to stress.

Motor Skill Coordination and Development

You should point out that the primary school years represent a crucially important time for the development of basic physical skills and motor coordination. The secondary school phase is too late for many, as numerous adults (including perhaps some of your colleagues) know from experience. For example if a child has difficulty in throwing, catching and hitting a ball, is unable to stay afloat in the swimming pool, cannot respond to a simple skipping rhythm and so on, the possibilities of joining with others in various pay activities become increasingly limited. This can cause great distress to a child.

Furthermore, they are being denied a source of great pleasure and satisfaction.

There is also the safety aspect to consider, not only in relation to water but also to the outdoors where climbing, balance and general motor coordination are important factors. You could remind teachers that every child is entitled to the opportunity to develop his or her own special talents and for some, these will be in the physical domain.

Personal and Social Development

PE is an area of the curriculum where all children can achieve success and merit genuine praise, which are fundamental factors in the development of a positive self image. However, you may find that many teachers consider this is relevant only to children who have difficulties with class work. You need to stress the importance of achieving success in at least one physical activity for the self esteem of *all* children, including those whose natural abilities are not in the physical domain. Some of these pupils may have no problems in other aspects of the curriculum. Other beneficial effects of PE experiences should also be pointed out, such as the numerous opportunities for children to cooperate, share equipment and so on.

Cognitive Development

You may need to remind teachers that PE is a combination of both the physical and the cognitive. Children are constantly required to make decisions, devise solutions to problems, select, observe, plan, judge, adapt, reflect, and so PE experiences make substantial contribution to cognitive development. Physical exercise also has an invigorating effect on the whole being, releasing tensions and in this way helping classroom learning.

You could make teachers aware of research in the USA, such as the work of Kephart, Frostig and Maslow, which claims that there is a direct relationship between certain sensori-motor experiences, such as those offered by gymnastics and dance, and cognitive development. These authors argue that PE should be given a high priority with experience additional to any statutory requirements. Less controversial perhaps is the claim that the physical exploration of certain concepts, such as those of a spatial nature (up, down, right, left and so on), helps children to understand the relevant verbal and written symbols.

Aesthetic Development

The potential of PE for aesthetic development may not have occurred to many of your teachers. Perhaps they associated 'aesthetic' with dance, or the arts, or merely 'beauty'. The manner of a performance, doing something well, enjoying physical activity both as a participant and an observer, *just for its own sake* are all aesthetic considerations. You may find that stressing the value of the quality of movement appeals to many primary teachers who feel that the competitive aspect of PE should be modified, particularly with young children. Becoming more aware of our environment is also an aesthetic aspect of outdoor and adventurous activities.

Creative Development

Opportunities to devise games, gymnastic sequences and dances also contribute to creative development. Point out that the creative process of experimentation, selection, rejection, is present in virtually every PE lesson. Furthermore the child as a whole person as involved, physically, cognitively and emotionally, making such creative experiences particularly valuable.

Staff need to debate the absolutely fundamental question:

WHY TEACH PE?

Some coordinators have found that presenting arguments (such as those given above) helps to clarify for teachers the overall AIM of PE. Guided by you, and after thorough discussions, the following conclusion or a similar one may be reached:

The overall aim of the PE curriculum is the integrated physical, motor skill, personal and social, aesthetic and creative development of each child.

Games, gymnastics, dance, athletics, swimming, outdoor and adventurous activities, contribute to this integrated all-round development of the child. However teachers, headteachers and governors may also need to be convinced of the specific value of each activity, that is, the

Objectives

Gymnastics

Gymnastics is concerned with the control and safe management of the body through creative-skill experiences; endurance, coordination, strength, mobility, flexibility, resilience and balance can be improved; the aesthetic aspect, (how a movement is performed) is integral to the activity. There is also the possibility of specific contributions to cognitive growth by means of distinctive perceptual motor experiences.

Games

Games are an important aspect of our culture. It is essential that children develop basic knowledge, skills and understanding for their social and personal development. Regular participation develops and maintains cardiovascular fitness, contributes to cognitive development, creativity and an appreciation of the aesthetic aspects of sport a valuable antidote to the 'win at all costs' approach.

Dance

Dance offers extensive opportunities for aesthetic and creative development by means of the expression and communication of feelings and ideas through movement; learning to use movement symbols, in addition to those of language and other arts, extends the range of expressive possibilities for each child; dance is also a useful means of gaining fitness, mobility and coordination, as well as releasing tension, developing rhythmical skills and basic spatial awareness.

Swimming

Swimming is primarily about survival, for we live on an island with innumerable lakes, rivers, and canals; inability to swim also excludes involvement in water sports such as sailing, canoeing, surfing, water-sking and so on. However, swimming also provides excellent all-round exercise and recreation which can be enjoyed throughout life; all children can participate fully, regardless of physical or cognitive ability.

Athletics

Athletics can improve cardiovascular health, flexibility, suppleness, muscular strength, endurance, athletic experience contributes to the development of games skills such as running, dodging and jumping.

Outdoor and adventurous activities

Outdoor and adventurous activities develop stamina, perseverance and endurance; children learn to respond safely to challenges presented by different environments; they learn to assess situation and cooperate with others. A respect for the environment and in aesthetic appreciation can also be encouraged.

Convincing your colleagues, headteacher and governors of the importance of PE in the all-round development of the child may be a necessary first step towards achieving a whole-school approach to the PE curriculum. At the same time you need to know where you are starting from and what your priorities will be.

A PE CURRICULUM AUDIT

Chapter One outlined the various means of acquiring basic information and background knowledge, including asking questions, observing and being generally aware of relevant facilities and opportunities — both within the school and in the community. It was stressed that you need to be open about what you are doing and careful that you do not raise the profile of this curriculum area too soon.

The National Curriculum Council's *Framework for the Primary Curriculum* poses a number of questions which may be useful in gaining a general, overall view of the current PE provision in your school.

— What do children do in various classes?

— What is missing?

— How does it compare with the requirements of the National Curriculum?

— What gaps can be easily filled?

— What action will be needed to fill them?

An initial task is to check on the extent, state of repair and stability of the facilities, apparatus, equipment and other essential resources for the teaching of each aspect of PE. In this way your can identify immediate and long-term needs.

You then need to talk to your headteacher and teachers. Remember that you will need to be diplomatic as they could be feeling insecure and perhaps defensive when discussing this aspect of the curriculum. You should also bear in mind that information can be collected over a period of time by means of both informed casual conversations and more formal meetings.

Ask the Staff

— Which aspects of PE are taught?

— Are some areas neglected and others over-emphasised?

— Is there any interest or expertise in any aspect?

— In what areas do individuals feel most or least confident?

— How much familiarity do teachers have with the National Curriculum PE document and requirements for relevant age groups?

— Is there one overall scheme of work and if so, is it implemented?

— If there are individual schemes of work do they relate to each other and to an overall school approach?

— Is there a common lesson plan for each activity?

— Is there consistency in organisation and handling of equipment and teaching approaches?

— How is children's progress assessed and recorded?

— Is there any liaison between teachers? Are teachers aware of each other's work?

— How do teachers cater for equality of access and opportunity in terms of gender, special educational needs and ethnic minorities?

— Is any provision made for multicultural education?

Ask your Headteacher

— What funding will you be allocated for resources and equipment?

— Is any existing school or LEA documentation available on the PE curriculum including policy statements, schemes of work, safety guidelines, assessments, record keeping?

— What timetable arrangements will be made to meet the requirements of the National Curriculum?

— What provision will be made for swimming? Will any Outdoor Activities residential experience be possible?

— What provision is currently made to ensure equality of opportunity in terms of gender, special educational needs and ethnic minorities?

— What is the current policy on multicultural education?

— Can you expect full support in the development of your own knowledge, skills and understanding?

— What non-contact time will you get for staff development including meetings and observing good practice outside school?

— Are other forms of school INSET possible such as demonstration lessons by you and team teaching?

— What priorities does he or she have as far as the PE curriculum is concerned?

By discussing the current provision for PE with your headteacher and staff — while gently informing them of the valuable contributions PE can make to the all-round education and development of the child — you will promote the growth of a shared understanding of and commitment to this area of the curriculum. Collective staff deliberation could them produce a school policy statement on PE. Such a statement might be:

We believe that PE can provide valuable integrated educational experiences. We are committed to the provision of a broad, balanced and differentiated PE curriculum which is progressive, stimulating and challenging for pupils for all abilities and backgrounds.

This establishers an overall sense of purpose and direction.

THE NATIONAL PE CURRICULUM

The Stationary and Non-Statutory Guidance for PE in the National Curriculum will be the focus of your planning. You will need to be fully familiar with these requirements in order to convey the main points to your colleagues. Remember that teachers are already overwhelmed with details from eight other subjects, so you need a restrict information to the essentials.

What Teachers Need to Know

— Begin with the good news — there are no SATS.

Assessment will be continues and based on the teachers's observation. Recording will be straightforward, using simple criteria which should be supplied by you, the curriculum coordinator.

— There is just one Attainment Target and this is expressed in the Key Stage statements. These aim to develop knowledge, skills and understanding by means of performing, composing and evaluating.

— There are three parts to the Programmes of Study:

  1. For everyone across all four Key Stages.
  2. General Programme of Study for Key Stage 1 and Key Stage 2.
  3. Activity Specific for Key Stage 1 and Key Stage 2.

— Primary PE comprises six activities but the central aspects are games, gymnastics and dance.

— Athletics is catered for mainly in games lessons with more specific teaching towards the end of Key Stage 2.

— The outdoor and adventurous activities area has close links with geography and science.

— All children should be able to swim at least twenty-five metres at the end of Key Stage 2.

— The emphasis is on physical activity but the cognitive aspect is underlined. Children must be aware of the process, i.e. to 'plan, do and review'.

What You as PE Curriculum Leader Need to Know, Find Out and Develop

— Aim to become thoroughly familiar with the requirements for each activity at Key Stage 1 and Key Stage 2 and know when each comes into effect. This will be essential for your planning, organisation, ordering of resources and so on.

— Examine the Programme of Study and the associated sections of Key Stage statements 1 and 2, and identify gaps in your existing provision.

- Compare Key Stage 1 and Key Stage 2 statements nothing the progression required.
- Identify the broad areas of assessment by studying relationship of the Key Stage statement to the POS.
- Compose simple criteria using the Key Stage statement and other schemes will be helpful here.
- Consider to what extent cross-curricular skills and themes can be implemented in PE.
- Investigate the possible contribution aspects of PE can make to learning in other curriculum areas.

DEVELOPING A WHOLE-SCHOOL APPROACH TO PE

Ascertaining current provision for PE, the production of a school policy statement, discussions with staff on the National Curriculum requirements, are all necessary precursors in the development of a whole-school approach to PE.

A whole-school approach is centred on:

- Continuity
- Progression
- Consistency.

It is your responsibility as the curriculum coordinator, to ensure that each of these happens and you will also be helping staff to improve their PE teaching. However, you should not be expected to design a curriculum package based on these principles on your own. On the contrary, staff should be involved from the beginning in developing schemes of work, contributing ideas for lesson content and so on. In this way, everyone has a vested interest in the successful implementation of the whole curriculum.

Continuity, progression and consistency are, of course, interrelated but for the sake of clarity each will be dealt with separately here. In practice your aim will be to make advances in all three areas, the rate of development will depend upon your individual circumstances.

PLANNING FOR CONTINUITY IN THE PE PROGRAMME

You need to work towards ensuring continuity between classes. As pupils move from one year to the next, there should be no unplanned break in PE provision and no unnecessary repetition of previous work. Any overlap should be deliberately designed to reinforce learning and increase knowledge, skills and understanding.

AS PE coordinator you need to take an overall view in order to relate whole-school planning to individual schemes of work. You therefore need to develop, in close consultation with each teacher, a specific plan which is in harmony with the general school policy on PE, the National Curriculum statements of attainment and Programme of Study and any existing or developing systems of assessment and record keeping. The scheme should be as clear and straightforward as possible.

What should you include in a PE scheme of work?

— Relevant subject matter in terms of knowledge, skills and experiences appropriate for each age group and each activity. You should focus particularly on the central activities of the PE Curriculum, namely games, gymnastics and dance.

— Associated resources for each aspect of PE. For instance, suitable poems and music for different dance experiences, gymnastic apparatus and appropriate games activities.

— Sample lesson plans showing organisation and development, again for each activity.

— Appropriate teaching techniques and organisation incorporating relevant safety procedures.

— Arrangements for ensuring the provision for equality of access and opportunity in terms of gender, special educational needs, and ethnic minority groups.

— Indicate how cross-curricular skills and themes can be developed.

— Suggestions for topic work. You should consult with other curriculum coordinators and bear in mind any opportunities for multicultural education.

— Assessment. Indicate clearly what is to be assessed and include a simple, straightforward record sheet. An example of a self appraisal sheet for the children might also be included. This might comprise two or three statements, such as:

What I enjoy in PE;

What I don't enjoy'

What I think I'm good at.

— Timetable. This may vary each term. Swimming, for instance, may feature in a particular part of the year whereas weekly lessons are desirable in games, gymnastics and dance.

As well as closely involving every teacher in the development of their own scheme, you should also try to ensure that everyone is fully aware of how that scheme fits into the overall school document. You and the staff must also monitor schemes on a regular basis and be prepared to modify them where necessary.

PLANNING FOR PROGRESSION

Firstly you need a good understanding of what progression in PE means. This will arise from your own increasing knowledge of the subject area and your growing familiarity with the National PE Curriculum. You need to look closely at Key Stage statements 1 and 2 which summarise the progression expected between the ages of seven and eleven so that you can explain these to teachers. You may also need to devise intermediate goals.

You should work with teachers on improving their:

— knowledge and understanding of PE;

— ability to assess;

— organisational strategies and teaching techniques.

Knowledge and understanding of PE

View this as a priority but aim at a gradual improvement. Subject knowledge is a critical factor in the ability to assess progress and use appropriate, purposeful, affective organisational strategies and teaching techniques.

Focus on the basis principles of each activity to start with. Simplify and make everything as easy as possible.

Gymnastics

Gymnastics is about developing skilled body actions both on the floor and on apparatus. Travelling on the feet, on hands and feet, by rolling, climbing, pushing and pulling; jumping and landing safely; stillness and balance, swinging and hanging from apparatus. These actions are varied by changing dynamics and the use of space. Actions are linked together to form phrases and phrases combined to make sequences of increasing complexity.

Games

Games teaching is concerned with the acquisition of basic skills - running, jumping, dodging, marking, throwing, catching, kicking, heading, dribbling, serving, bowling, hitting, rolling, bouncing, aiming, trapping, intercepting, tackling, fielding — and developing an understanding of what is meant by playing a game.

Dance

In dance lessons the teacher aims to develop a wide range of expressive movements by extending the use of the body, space and dynamics. Children are also helped to compose dances which express feelings and ideas. Dances can be simple phrases or more complex compositions. A variety of stimuli are used in each case including different types of music, words and poems, percussive and other sounds.

Ability to Assess

There are no SATs for PE. Teachers will therefore need to know what to look for in order to recognise progress and difficulties. In PE a child's knowledge, skills and understanding are revealed in the quality of his or her:

- practical skilled *performances* in various activities;
- *compositions*, for instance games, sequences and dances devised;
- *evaluations* of personal performances and compositions as well as those of others.

PE is therefore a predominately practical subject and so the key assessment tool is *Observation*. However, children's own descriptions, comments and observations — including those in response to questions — will also provide valuable information. This will reveal their ability to evaluate and their level of understanding of the learning processes involved.

Good observational skills are nevertheless crucial and these will only develop over time. For most teachers, assessing progress in PE is likely to be a completely new experience and so practice and guidance will be required. You must help teachers to focus on important aspects. You will find that Rudolf Laban's analysis in terms of *Body*, *Space*, *Dynamics* and *Relationships* very helpful. You will also find helpful advice in the National Curriculum Council's Non-Statutory Guidance for PE.

Organisational Strategies and Teaching Techniques

The lesson plan is fundamentally important and the clear framework for PE is a distinct advantage. Furthermore, *organisational strategies* relating to individual, whole class and group teaching tie in closely with the lesson plan, for each is generally most appropriate at different stages of the lesson. Teachers are likely to need particular help and support from you in the use of gymnastic apparatus.

Teachers will also need to know what the *major teaching techniques* are in PE and when each is employed. In the past there has been little teacher intervention during PE lessons. You will need to help teachers to learn to use questioning, demonstrations, explanations, instructions, comments, suggestions and so on, both appropriately and with purpose.

How can you improve teachers' knowledge and understanding their assessment abilities and their employment of appropriate organisational strategies and teaching techniques? You should discuss the following suggestions with your headteacher and teachers so that priorities can be identified. You can then processed with their full cooperation and approval.

— Concentrate initially on gymnastics, games and dance. It may be useful to focus on each activity in turn rather than trying to improve teaching in all three simultaneously.

— Videotape recording, featuring specific activities, can provide an invaluable teaching aid for the PE coordinator. At the end of this chapter you will find details of videotapes on various aspects of PE which are available for sale and for hire. Whether illustrating a single lesson or taking a more general view, videotapes can be used to instruct and provoke discussions when issues can be raised and anxieties dealt with. Videotapes are a versatile teaching aid, for sections can be repeated easily enabling you to illustrate key aspects relating to subject matters, organisation, teaching techniques and evidence of progress. You need to be fully familiar with the contents of a videotape yourself before using it with teachers. Carefully prepare sessions before and be clear about your objectives.

— You may find that the occasional demonstration lesson by you for one or more teachers might be helpful. Again, the specific purpose must be clear to all concerned. Additionally — or as an alternative — some kind of them teaching could be employed. Within any one lesson the teacher(s) could be given varying degrees of responsibility depending on their individual needs. Ensure that they are fully involved at all times and not standing around 'like spare parts'.

— Some coordinators have found that a visit to observe work in another school is useful. Once again, you and the teachers should be clear on the purpose and choose the school with care. Remember that insecure staff may not be able to relate to very advanced work, it can seem to so far out of reach that it has a negative effect. On the other hand it is essential that only good practice is observed, so consult either with your LEA's PE advisor or perhaps a PE expert in a local Institute of Higher Education. In any case, you should have discussions with your counterpart in the school concerned before a visit.

— A PE advisor or PE specialist may be able to visit your school to discuss issues with staff, give demonstration lessons and so on. Such occasions need careful preparation to promote maximum benefit for all concerned. There may also be courses available locally which are relevant to your teachers' needs. Remember that you could make suggestions to PE specialists employed by your LEA or by a local Institute of Higher Education, thereby initiating the kind of course you want rather than just waiting for one to happen.

PLANNING FOR CONSISTENCY

To achieve consistency in the implementation of the PE curriculum, the coordinator must work towards agreement among all members of staff on a number of important basic issues. You must therefore be prepared to lead discussions and give advice. Take into account guidelines from your LEA and professional associations, such as the Physical Education Association, in order to gain consensus on the following:

- the way pupils dress for PE, including appropriate footwear. Staff footwear should also be considered;
- the correct method of handling, flexing, checking and using apparatus in various activities;
- the general teaching approach and employment of organisational strategies;
- rules concerning safe conduct within various PE activities;
- the recording of teachers' assessments of pupil progress;
- provision for children with Special Educational Needs in PE, including those with impairments and those from ethnic minority groups;
- equality of both access and opportunity in all aspects of PE.

You might also stress that many of these issues are of central importance in ensuring safe practice in PE, so agreement among staff concerning these procedures is particularly crucial. On the other hand, guard against alarming your teachers. Many are often unduly cautions particularly when large apparatus is involved, thereby limiting their pupils' experiences and restricting their development. For those children with natural ability in this area of the curriculum such extreme caution can be very frustrating. Underline the positive. Complying with safety procedures is an important part of PE for children. Sensible, safe conduct opens up opportunities for teacher and pupils alike.

Finally, remember that agreement among staff on the above issues should not be regarded as immutable. Procedures might need to be modified or added to in the light of experience.

THE SCHOOL PE DOCUMENT

You should aim to produce a PE document which brings together the major components referred to in this chapter, thus presenting an overall picture to your headteacher and teachers, and illustrating the whole-school approach to PE. Such a document would include the following information headings and be available for consultation:

- The school policy statement;
- Overall scheme of work;
- School PE timetable;
- Agreed safety procedures;
- Provision for equality of both access and opportunity;
- Sample lesson plans;
- Resources available for each activity;
- Equipment inventory;
- Current information on INSERT, facilities and expertise in the local community.

Compiling this document may seem an enormous task but remember that it will be built up gradually. In effect you will be merely consolidating in a written form, the results of the various discussions with your headteacher and the staff. Once you have the basic document in place you can then make changes, additions, and so on.

- Make the teaching of PE as easy as possible for the staff.
- Supply sample lesson plans.
- Organise and label boxes of PE equipment.
- Indicate clearly where gymnastic apparatus is stored in the hall.
- Make available simple record sheets.

As a PE coordinator considerable demands will be placed on you, but the rewards are commensurate with the efforts. The following quotation should sustain you:

At the heart of the process is the individual child who is entitled to the same opportunity to receive a broad, balanced, differentiated curriculum regardless of race, gender, disability or geographical location.

— *A Framework for the Primary Curriculum,* p. 10

A PROFESSIONAL DEVELOPMENT DAY IN PHYSICAL EDUCATION

Achieving a whole-school approach to PE and helping your colleagues to improve their teaching of the subject is the aim of everything discussed in this chapter. Finding the necessary time to work with staff can be a problem. If you are fortunate enough to be given a whole day for staff development, then, you will want to maximise what could be a rare opportunity. A great deal of progress can be made when the staff's focus of attention is entirely on aspects of PE teachings.

The basic considerations you need to take into account when planning a professional development day for your colleagues have been outlined earlier. It would be useful for you to consult that section before proceeding. You will see that thorough preparation is absolutely essential for success.

Clarify Your Purpose For the Day

Let us imagine that from your discussion with staff an introduction to gymnastics teaching is regarded by them as a priority. More specifically they would like to observe infant and junior lessons which illustrate fundamental principles of gymnastics teaching and basic organisation. They are particularly apprehensive about the apparatus section of the lesson. Not surprisingly there is some anxiety about the National Curriculum. Some guidance on what will be expected of them is needed.

Begin to Plan

The needs of the staff suggest that a school-based day will best meet their requirements. We will assume that classes of children will not be available for you to give demonstration lessons. A suitable videotape must be ordered such as the made by Manchester Education Committee (details are available at the end of this chapter). Incidentally, if children are available, must of what follows will still apply. There are obvious disadvantages in relying on videotaped lessons, but also advantages. For instance, the whole lesson can be observed and then rewound to focus on particular sections. The tape can be stopped or slowed down so that you can emphasises a specific point. You can also return to the videotape if necessary during subsequent discussions.

However it is essential to make yourself thoroughly familiar with both the videotape and, of course, the video machine. Check that the machine is in good working order and there are back-up facilities if necessary. Make a note of the major points you want to stress in each of the lessons, and — most important — note the machine' numbers! This is vital so that you can rewind it to the sections you need.

In order to familiarise staff with gymnastic apparatus, a workshop is probably the best approach where actually set out apparatus arrangements suitable for infants and for juniors. In this way you will be able to stress the safety factors, correct handling and appropriate storage. Remember to reassure staff at an early stage that they will not have to actually *do* any gymnastics themselves.

Plan the Detail

1. Decide on the structure of the day. The morning sessions is usually the best time for the major work of the day, so the videotapes and associated discussions should take place then. Apparatus work could be planned for the afternoon.

A possible timetable might be:

9.00-9.30 Introduction

Outline the purpose of the day. Reassure staff yet again that they will not be asked to do any gymnastics themselves.

Explain the basics of gymnastics teaching as simply as possible.

9.30-9.45 Introduce the videotape. Explain what it comprises, where it was made (Manchester in this particular instance) and so on.

9.45-10.30 Videotape of infant lesson. Discussion. Indicate how the work seen relates to National Curriculum requirements.

10.30-10.50 Coffee break.

10.50-12.00 Videotape of junior gymnastics lesson. Discussion. Relate the work seen to National Curriculum requirements.

12.00-1.00 Lunch.

1.00-2.15 Workshop on the introduction, organisation and safe handling of apparatus.

2.15-2.45 Tea.

2.45-3.3.0 Final discussion and evaluation.

You would of course need to discuss any proposed timetable with your headteacher and then perhaps circulate it to the staff for their reaction.

2. You should prepare a number of hand-outs for the staff which you can distribute at appropriate points in the day. Remember to keep information to the minimum. Closely typed pages will put your teachers off immediately.

You should have available copies of:

— the final agreed plan of the day;
— the fundamental principles of gymnastics teaching; the basic actions, building phrases and sequences, safety measures;
— outlines of the videotaped lessons they will see. Focus on the Objectives and the Structure of the lessons in each case. Indicate the main teaching points you will highlight;
— clear and simple apparatus plans for infants and for juniors. Safety aspects relating to the organisation, handling and storage of apparatus;
— National Curriculum requirements of Key Stage 1 and Key Stage 2. Select and summarise the relevant sections for gymnastics.

Running the Day

Take not of the helpful advice offered in Chapter Two. Remember to check that you videotape machine is working. Then after all your hard work — enjoy the day!

Taking Stock

Once again, the suggestions made in the earlier chapter are useful and your should act on the advice given there. For instance, make a note of the major outcomes of the day. Subsequent discussions with your headteacher and the staff will help you to plan the next stage.

The prospect of organising and running a professional development day for your colleagues can be daunting. You will probably find that the staff are very sympathetic, as many will be or have been in a similar situation as coordinators for other subjects. They are also likely to be anxious about their limited knowledge of PE. Your through preparation will ensure that staff are not wasting their time, and you will have gained invaluable experience. It will be much easier next time!

REFERENCES AND RESOURCES

The following publications are referred to in this chapter:

Alexander, R., Rose, J., Woodhead, C. *Curriculum Organisation and Classroom Practice in Primary Schools,* DES, London, 1992.

Calouste Gulbenkian Foundation. *The Arts in the Primary School,* London, 1989.

Frostig, M. and Maslow, P. *Learning Problems in the Classroom,* Grune and Stratton, New York, 1973.

Kepart, N.C. The *Slow Learner in the Classroom,* Charles Merrill, Columbus, Ohio, 1960.

National Curriculum Council. *Physical Education in the National Curriculum,* York, 1991.

National Curriculum Council. *Physical Education. Non-Statutory Guidance,* York, 1992.

Physical Education Association. *Report of a Commission of Enquiry,* Ling House, London, 1987.

Sanderson, P. *Physical education and dance.* In T. Roberts (ed.) *Encouraging Expression. Arts in the primary school,* Cassell, London, 1988.

You will find that this chapter also gives valuable overviews of PE curriculum content, progression, teaching techniques, organisation, safety aspects and special needs.

Two Curriculum Leader's handbooks published by LEAs are

useful particularly for lesson planning and content, lists of suppliers of equipment, curriculum text books and so on:

Hereford and Worcester County Council. *The Physical Education Curriculum Leader's Handbook,* Worcester, 1991.

Jones, B. *Curriculum Leadership in Physical Education,* Durham LEA and University of Newcastle upon Tyne, 1990.

If possible you or your school should join The Physical Education Association of Great Britain and Northern Ireland, Ling House, 162 Kings Cross Road, London, WCIX 9DH. This professional organisation publishes to journals, *The British Journal of Physical Education* and *Primary PE focus,* which include valuable information on current developments, curriculum materials, conferences, and other resources.

There may also be a local PE association which you could join where you would make contact with other curriculum coordinators, share ideas, receive advice, support and information.

Another useful organisation for you to contact is the Central Council for Physical Recreation (CCPR), Francis House, Francis Street, London, SWIP IDG.

For dance specifically contact the Education Unit, The Arts Council, Piccadilly, London, W1. Regional Arts Associations can also be helpful.

Additional sources of information on the dance curriculum include the journal *Drama and Dance* promoted by Leicester Education Committee, and available from AB Printers Ltd, 33 Cannock Street, Leicester, LE4 7HR.

BBC Educational Publishing, PO Box 234, Wetherby, West Yorkshire, LS23 7EU produces very good tapes of music for dance as well as booklets on dance ideas. The National Dance Teachers' Association, Islington Sixth form Centre, Benwell Road, London, N7 7BW produces a useful journal *Dance Matters.*

You will probably find that your own LEA has produced guidelines on various aspects of the PE curriculum. LEAs whose publications are particularly useful include those of the City of Coventry, Elm Bank Teacher's Centre, Mile Lane, Coventry, CV1 2WN and Staffordshire Country Council, PE Section, Education Offices, Tipping Street, Stafford, ST16 2DH.

The following are suppliers of videotapes and films for sale or hire, on various aspects of the PE curriculum: DS Information System Limited NAVAL, The Art Building, Normal College (Top Site), Siliwen Road, Bangor, Gwynned, LL57 2DZ and Concord Video and Film Council, 201 Felixtowe Road, Ipswich, IP3 9BJ.

A videotape on teaching dance in the primary school is available on free loan from: BBC School Radio Cassette Service, Broadcasting House, London, W1A 1AA. Primary school gymnastics is the subject of a videotape produced by Manchester Education Committee in association which Continental Sports Products Company, Paddock, Huddersfield, HD1 4SD. The latter is also a well-established supplier of PE equipment.

9

THE GEOGRAPHY IN THE PRIMARY SCHOOL

WHAT IS GEOGRAPHY?

Coordinators find that teachers' ideas about the nature of geography vary considerably. Getting the staff of the school together to compare idaes has proved a useful start to discussion. Some of the responses to this question are given by teachers, and those intending to teach geography, in the primary school.

Geography is:

'the study of people and places and the way in which they interact with the environment';

'studying a child's immediate environment and developing from that a deeping knowledge about people and places that are far away';

'looking at maps, land forms, weather, climate and why people behave in a certain way in relation to where they live and why they live there'.

As teacher' ideas about the nature of geography will vary, getting the staff together to compare ideas will be a useful start to discussion. In this way, the responses that the staff make and their perceptions about geography can be shared. They can then go on together to produce a definition of geography which is close to that given in the Non-Statutory Guidance for Teachers:

Geography explores the relationship between the earth and its peoples. It studies the location of the physical and human features of the earth and the processes, systems and inter-relationships that create and influence them. The character of places, the subject's central focus, derives from the interaction of people and environments.

Curriculum Council for Wales 1991

Teachers will feel that they own a definition of geography themselves that might be very similar to this.

WHY TEACH GEOGRAPHY IN THE PRIMARY SCHOOL?

Over the past twenty to thirty year and throughout the great debate towards the National Curriculum and beyond, we can see an increasing need for teachers to be accountable for what they teach and also how it is taught. Teaching a subject because it is now the law can therefore provide an answer to the above question, but this is rather a narrow one. The curriculum coordinator for geography, and the staff as a whole, need to be clear about the aims of geographical education and how these aims fit in to the school's overall curriculum policy.

A helpful quote when discussing the school's aims and objectives for geography is taken from HMT's *Geography from* 5-16 which suggests that studying.

Geography helps pupils to make sense of their surroundings and to gain a better appreciation and understanding of the variety of physical and human conditions on the earth's surface. It has direct relevance for pupils aged from 5-16 because it relates to many aspects of their own lives and of the environment in which they live.

(p. 1, para. 1)

Discussion along these lines can be used by you, the coordinator, to produce a written statement of aims and objectives for geography in accordance with the school's overall policy statement. This could lead you to draw up an agreed school policy document for geography. It will need to contain both a scheme of work, which clearly shows the place of geography, and a Key Stage plan, together with clearly laid out unit or topic plans.

In drawing up a policy document it is essential that the views of the whole of the staff in the school are considered. Borrowing a policy document from another school, or writing it without consultation with others is likely to lead to a policy on paper only; its ideas will not take root in classroom practice. If members of staff have contributed their ideas, then it is likely that the policy document will give a true picture of current and future work in geography. As coordinator, writing a policy document will largely be left to you. It is important to arrange a series of consultation meetings to enable agreement to be reached. When writing the policy document, it is helpful to imagine that your audience is a new member of staff so that everything you include is both helpful and in keeping with the ethos of the school.

The school geography policy document will vary a great deal from school to school but it might contain:

- a written statement showing the aims and objectives for geography;
- a Key Stage plan;
- a topic or unit plan which shows the place of geography within the whole curriculum;
- a description of how assessment in geography is linked to the school's overall assessment policy;
- a list of available resources;
- a plan sharing details of resources to be obtained in the future;
- a list of places where members of staff can get help, such as local planning officers, Country Records Offices;
- a list of suitable places for class visits;
- details of the agreed school recording system for children's progress in geography;
- details of the local secondary schools syllabus for geography in Y7;
- a timetable for appropriate TV broadcasts; and a list of suitable books, both fiction and non-fiction, with a geographical content;
- a schedule for the evaluation review of the policy.

In asking and answering the question, 'What is Geography?' not only will you and the rest of the staff have clearer picture of what geography is all about, but you will also be part way towards writing (or revising if necessary), your policy document. Another important question for the coordinator to ask concerns the assessment of the current situation in your school.

HOW MUCH GEOGRAPHY IS TAKING PLACE IN MY CLASSROOM AND MY SCHOOL?

This is a very important question for any coordinator to ask. It is the first stage towards the process of change mentioned in Chapter One.

Before any learning can take place, an accurate assessment of the present situation is vital to determine the next step. Some teachers teach geography as an isolated subject, but the interrelated nature of primary curriculum subjects means that some geography is likely to be taught in association with other areas of the curriculum. Hence, there may be more geography taught than is realised. During meetings, coordinators may use the discussion of the geography that takes place in one particular classroom, perhaps the coordionator's own, to help other teachers to recognise the many facets of geography that take place in their classroom.

INSET ACTIVITY

Starting points might be:

- to persuade one teacher to discuss the geographical aspect of an activity or topic they have carried out with children;
- to watch a video together showing children working on a project, such as the BBC video *Teaching Today;*
- to show colleagues some of the work that the children in your class have been doing;
- to invite a teacher from another school to show the geographical work that they have been involved in with their class.

As one reception teacher remarked after watching a video session:

'I've been taking like this to my four year olds for the past twenty years but I didn't realise properly until today that I was doing so much geography'.

She was referring to the language she used when she showed children how to tidy away equipment.

Another teacher of an upper junior class announced:

'I've read that novel to classes on many occasions but I'd never realised the full geographical potential within it'.

She was referring to the noval *My side of the Mountain* by J. George.

In both instances the teachers had been covering aspects of geography which children but needed to be made more aware of how to focus on the elements which were specifically geographical.

During an INSET activity you will be gathering informally lot of information about the extent to which geography is covered in the school. This, together with any information you have gained by asking questions and collecting evidence, should lead you to the next step which is to ask the following question.

HOW CAN THE NEEDS OF THE SCHOOL BE EVALUATED?

A full evaluation of the school's needs can only be achieved when all the staff are involved. Your role as geography coordinator is to take a leading part in the development of the school's geography policy. This will assist the headteacher and staff considerably. It is not necessary for you to have a professional qualification in geography. It is more important that you display enthusiasm for the subject and are prepared to find our more about it.

As each school is different, it is not possible to offer prescriptive advice. The needs of the school will change over time and every teacher will have individual needs. Some schools have a detailed policy for the professional development of their staff, others may have less experienced members of staff who need more help, some may have staff who need to be encouraged to alter some of their ideas about how children can best learn geography. In every case, however, it is very important that staff exchange ideas about the most effective ways to teach geography. Tried and tested methods can prove to be the most valid — sometimes new ideas are taken on board without their methods being fully comprehended. What has to be decided is how the teachers can best enable their children to learn geography.

In order to help coordinators and teachers identify their task, we will give some examples of how some geography coordinators tackled their own problems.

One coordinator assessed the situation in school and asked the teachers themselves what they felt their needs were. This formed the basis for a plan of action. At the time the staff were very involved in incorporating geography into a National Curriculum framework. They felt that any geography INSET should be relevant as their time was very precious.

The teacher identified several needs:

— They felt they needed to work out how geography fitted into the primary curriculum so that children's interests and experiences were extended.

— They wanted to look at how geographical concepts, knowledge and skills could be taught. They felt it was important that they received in-service training on how to teach physical geography.

— They specified that in looking at the geography of far away places, they needed to agree on the localities to be studied. They had to decide which locality in the European Community or economically developing country the school should look at.

— They needed to share their interpretation of the relevant documents (on this occasion the National Curriculum geography document) and clarify what certain terms meant.

— They were concerned that adequate resources should be provided. They wanted to extend the use of IT to support geographical work.

This was the feeling of the staff at one school. Such concerns might be common to many schools. You might use these as a starting point in a session with staff on a training day. We will take each point in turn and give suggestions for solutions.

How can geography be fitted into the curriculum so that the children's interests and experiences can be extended?

Organising a scheme of work for geography can be done in a variety of different ways. Some schools may prefer to devise a separate scheme for geography, others may wish to line the subject with science, history or adopt an approach where the subjects are fully integrated. The topic might be a geography focused topic or the geographical aspects may be taken out of a more general topic. Suggestions for this are contained in the Non-Statutory Guidance for Wales (Section C).

During the 1980s there was an upsurge in the quality and quantity of science taught in primary classrooms; many schools quite successfully used a science-based topic as a vehicle for the whole curriculum. The danger with this type of approach is that it could lead to an imbalance of subjects — particularly when core subjects are subject to statutory assessment whereas foundation subjects are not.

Geography has many links with science, most obviously those aspects of work concerned with weather and climate, and work based around rocks and the landscape. When aspects of the geography curriculum are included in a largely science focused topic, it is important to make teachers aware of other parts of the geography curriculum, especially AT's 2, 4 and 5 which provide a context for At 3, Physical Geography.

One coordinator of both history and geography helped to devise a whole-school plan to achieve a balanced curriculum and also to deal with some of the issues arising because the school had vertically grouped classes.

This focus demonstrates links between history and geography in three main areas:

— *content* — a study of the local area (this link diminishes rapidly in Key States 2 and 3).

— *conceptual overlap* — cause and effect, how places change, similarity and difference.

— enquiry.

In planning topics or units of work it is important to use these obvious links, whilst at the same time ensuring that a balanced curriculum is achieved. In the example each teacher took the terms or half-term topic and decided upon:

— what investigations the children were going to make and the questions that they might ask;

— the resources needed;
— skills to be acquired;
— knowledge and understanding to be gained and attitudes to be fostered;
— National Curriculum attainment targets involved.

In this way continuity throughout the school in terms of time allocation, general themes and organisation can be effectively achieved.

Planning also needs to take account of the importance of progression in skills and concepts. In mapping skills, for example, children move from the early stages of drawing plans and maps to the more detailed plans and maps of varying scale. As children progress through the school they need to develop their use of symbols, map keys and directional compasses. They become able to measure distance, scale up and down, and select routes. They develop their concepts of scale, location, routes and place. Furthermore, teachers need to be encouraged to build upon the geographical understanding that children already have when they come to school.

In this way the complexity of information and relationship was gradually increase. We start with what the child already knows and then progress from the child's immediate environment to the more distant places, from the particular to the more general and from the concrete to the abstract. A child does not suddenly develop a concept the first time he meets it. A concept emerges over a period of time. Planning for progression in geography needs to take account of Bruner's spiral curriculum and the importance of constant revision in order for the child's understanding of a concept to grow. For example, the concept of *location,* is something that needs particular attention.

Let us suppose, that as part of the topic on 'Homes' the teacher has brought a cage into school ready for a guinea pig. The infant class has to decide what the guinea pig will need in its cage and where the various items should be located. The animal will require warmth, security and a place to sleep. It will also need a supply of food and water in addition to a suitable place for a toilet. Even a very young child will understand the importance of locating these elements. When older children have to decide upon the positioning of a school garden, they will build upon what they learnt when they designed the guinea pig's

Reception	Ongoing Activities/Display Table Weather recording, nature walks, free play road mats, houses, model railways, shops, bricks, dressing up etc. Museum/far away table. Collection of artefacts. Topical themes.					
Year 1	Ourselves	Around and about our school	Dinosaurs	Change	Moving toys	A journey to
Year 2	Holidays	Grandad's Christmas	Food	Houses	Animals & Plants	Water
Year 3	Yr 1 Transport Yr 2 Homes		Yr 1 Weather Yr 2 Planet Earth			
Year 3-4	Yr 1 transport Yr 2 Homes		Yr 1 Weather Yr 2 Planet Earth		1991/92 Invaders and Settlers 1992/3 Tudors and Stuarts/	
Year 4-5	Yr 1 Growth	Energy/Light	History and Geography	Yr 1 Underground	Explorations and Encounters	
	Yr 2	Wider World	Local Study	Yr 2 Phys. Geog.		
Year 5	Yr 1 Growth	Energy/Light	History and Geography	Yr 1 Underground	1993/4 Victorians/Britain since 1930's	
	Yr 2	Wider World	Local Study	Yr 2 Phys. Geog.		
Year 5-6	Yr 1 Keeping Healthy	History and Geography	Yr 1 Going through the tunnel	River Study	1994/5 Ancient Civilisations (Egypt and Greece)	
	Yr 2 Space	Local Study	Yr 2 Wider World	The Landscape		
Year 6	Yr 1 Keeping Healthy	History and Geography	Yr 1 Going through the tunnel	River Study		
	Yr 2 Space	Local Study	Yr 2 Wider World	The Landscape		

Strands:		
	Mapping skills	Use of artefacts and primary resources
Knowledge and understanding of place	Use of atlas	Use of IT, CDT
Weather recording	Materials	

cage. In the same way, they will learn, at a later stage, to appreciate why their local school or supermarket was sited where it is and why their home town has its particular location.

Progression in geography takes place through the increased complexity and accuracy of skills used, the scale of the areas studied (from the local environment, through regions and countries, to international and global scales), and the complexity of the context in which the enquiry is done.

How can geographical skills and knowledge be taught?

Coordinators should need to convince their colleagues that it is by asking questions, examining evidence and attempting explanations that the child will be more likely to understand the various aspects of geography. It is not sufficient that children are told facts or research information merely from books, although their is obviously some place for this activity. In the same way, although published schemes can be used to teach geography they are not specifically written for one particular child or class. Obviously, they cannot replace practical activities taking place through first-hand enquiry, sometimes including fieldwork. Nothing can completely replace first-hand experience both inside and outside the classroom. An enquiry approach is very important with evidence collected in the field and investigated together with relevant secondary source material such as maps, photographs and printed materials.

Children learn best when they see that they are part of the phenomenon they are studying, so any topic should not be set apart from their lives or lives known to them. It therefore follows that children should be entitled to learn geography in an effective way. A skills-based course isolated from an enquiry into place and/or thematic geography is undesirable and is unlikely to give a balanced geography curriculum.

It is sometimes necessary, however, to spend time teaching a particular skill in order to continue with a branch of enquiry. Trying to show thirty-five children how to use a directional compass whilst it is blowing a gale on a hillside can be rather difficult! Children need to be shown how to use the compass in the classroom beforehand in order that they are able to use it in the field. The teacher must plan for this to take place. If the children are going on a field trip and have to know how to read on Ordnance Survey map then it makes more sense to look at the map of the area that they will be visiting rather than a map of the area surrounding a randomly chosen town in a geography textbook. This obviously has implications for resources.

Sometimes your colleagues will lack confidence in teaching geographical skills within an enquiry method. There is a definite need for concrete examples showing how this can be done. If the coordinator pilots a study they can share this study with others during an INSET day.

Examples of Geographical Enquiries using the local area and beyond.

Case One

Teacher and children make a study of their local area. They could choose to look at the school, the local shop, the local park etc. The children are encouraged to ask questions about the use of land, buildings, people and the effects of the weather. The process of geographical enquiry in which children identify features of their lives, the lives of others, or features of the environment, provides a basis for comparative studies of other areas. This is a requirement of the National Curriculum Geography orders. After studying one locality, they compare this area with another area, possibly by going on a school trip. In some cases the statutory requirement that the local area should be compared with a contrasting UK locality can be successfully achieved through 'twinning'. Many schools have used 'twinning', a process where a teacher 'twins' with another teacher in another area and children exchange information, resources, ides, examples of pieces of work. A visit to the other school can be you exciting and meaningful for children, and in collecting evidence from their own locality they have a clear purpose for their enquiry. Similarly, studying a locality beyond the UK can be enhanced if the school 'twins' with a school from abroad. One advantage of such arrangements is that there can be an extensive exchange of sources, including large scale maps and local information. Another advantage is that the children are working with resources that are similar to those their own.

If the resources appropriate to the needs of one class are collected then these can then be used by other colleagues in the school at a later date. The geography coordinator can assist by keeping an inventory of the resources available.

Case Two

Another geography coordinator took a class out on a field trip. She had a particular purpose in mind which had been discussed with the children beforehand. Even though there was a limit to the number of activities that she could successfully carry out, the enquiry had a clear focus. They climbed a nearby hill, and children and teacher together looked at features with the purpose of producing a map. The teacher pointed out the importance of map orientation and during their drawing the children realised the need to have a landmark at the top and bottom. They marked the position of shelter, noticed where the opening was and discussed what had influenced the position of the door of the shelter. The children used directional compasses and then tested the wind direction for a clear purpose. They wanted to find out if these factors had influenced the location of the shelter. The children produced annotated field sketches and used the information they had collected as the basis for work in the next few weeks.

Examples could form a stimulus for discussion as a part of an INSET day. This might also include the coordinator examining how they had carried out an enquiry, starting at the planning stage and then showing that the children had achieved with examples of their work. Alternatively the geography coordinator could plan similar enquiries of a first-hand nature through fieldwork, through secondary sources or a combination of the two. Colleagues may need you to help them with reading maps, producing a map, a field sketch, using surveying equipment, weather measuring equipment and directional compasses. This sort of activity would have to be carefully organised so that teachers would find it useful, non-threatening and a boost to confidence.

Teachers often need help in the area of teaching physical geography. Some are reluctant to ask, so the whole issue will need very careful handling. It could be appropriate for the geography coordinator to pilot an aspect of physical geography, such as a river study, and then share this with the rest of the staff.

It is important that with any INSET activities planned by the geography coordinator, the support and involvement of the headteacher, both in the planning stage and in actually taking part on the day, is seen by other members of staff. If an INSET day is to involve fieldwork then the involvement of parents and governors at this or at a later stage might be appropriate, but this would depend upon the confidence of the staff.

You do not need to travel far in order to teach physical geography. When using the local area, the setting of a school in an urban environment should not inhibit the teaching of physical geography. Infant children can investigate where water goes after heavy rain and junior children can investigate how storm water drains might run into a local stream. No area lacks physical features. By investigating the drainage on a new housing estate, the children can find out a great deal about how the landscape has been shaped by bulldozers when the houses were being built.

INSET ACTIVITY

To be effective, teacher assessment will need to be closely linked to the teaching and learning process. On an INSET day colleagues might find it useful to study the 'command words' used at the beginning of each Statement of Attainment and consider what applications these have for teaching, learning and assessing. For example *identifying* familiar features on photographs and pictures, *make* a map of a short route showing features in the correct order.

The school also needs to develop a policy for planning assessment and evaluating children's progress. This is an integral part of the planning process. How achievements are recorded and results reported to parents will have to be decided. This will be in line with the school's overall assessment policy and might include the use of Non-mandatory SATs. As coordinator, you will need to make sure all staff know what mechanisms are in place to asses, record and report on children's progress. If a general profile of each child is to be produced at the end of each year or Key Stage then the Geographical Accociation booklet profiling in *Geography,* edited by N. J. Greaves and M. Naish, may prove helpful. Though intended for secondary school teachers, the ideas may be useful to you as a geography coordinator in the primary school.

How can teachers develop children's concept of place to include knowledge and understanding of far away places? Children's experiences of space and place are fragmentary. It is part of the teacher's role as educator and enabler to build on these experiences. To the teacher the Lake District may conjure ideas of lakes, hills, valleys and glaciation; to the child it might be a trip in a hot car via the M6 motorway. Teachers need to find out what perceptions children have about any place they are to study. It may be that they have misconceptions based upon cultural stereotyping. One easy way to have some idea about how much children know is to get them to 'brainstorm' and tell you all they can about a particular locality. It is often surprising to discover where children's ideas come from. At the same time, it heightens teachers' awareness that the investigations which they carry out with the children need to be free from bias through gender, culture, race or any form of stereotyping.

INSET ACTIVITY

— Name a country and ask teachers to tell you everything that they know about that particular country. Write up these statements on a flip chart. Together, examine the set of responses and search for evidence of stereotyping.

— Collect a random selection of books with a largely geographical content from the school library. Use the same search methods you developed together for the previous task to look for examples of stereotyping.

This activity will help to develop teachers' awareness of the importance of checking that the books and materials they use in school are free from bias. Teachers also need to be aware that they may unconsciously influence their children in a biased way, and they must try to guard against this. The place of values and attitudes within the child's geographical education is an important one. As children study an economically developing county they could be dealing with issues of poverty or pollution. They will need to look at their own values and attitudes as well as those of others. The geography coordinator needs to ensure that the ways in which these issues are tackled are discussed adequately amongst the staff and decide whether some reference should be made to them in the geography policy document. Strategies for handling these can be obtained from the Development Education Project whose address appears at the end this chapter.

Handling similarities and differences in peoples or places has to be managed sensitively, particularly if the area where the child lives is not viewed in a positive way by others. By asking the children what they believe to be the positive attributes of where they live, teachers can avoid conveying their own, possible negative, perceptions to the children. Children might see many advantages of which others may not be aware.

Once children have an understanding of their own how area they are more likely to have a greater understanding of another child's home area. Choosing that area could be influenced by school visits, children's holidays or the teacher's interest. If the teacher has firsthand experience of another placed then it can help to bring that place alive for the children. Telling the story behind an artefact brought back from a distant place can be very exciting for children.

At Key Stage 1 the main emphasis is on a study of the local area but then extending it to another locality in the UK and later a locality in the wider world. Colleagues sometimes need to be reminded that it is the locality and not the whole country that is to be studied. Although this does not prevent the locality study leading to an awareness of the whole country or the child's general awareness of places throughout the wider world. At Key Stage 2 this general awareness increases though again the main emphasis is upon localscale studies leading to regional-scale work. A contrasting UK locality is studied as is a locality in an economically developing country. Choice of places will depend upon resources, pupil and teacher interest, and which places the children have studied previously.

Glossary of terms

A National Curriculum attainment targets and their purpose

Geographical skills (AT1) — those generic skills have a geographical context for their use application.

Knowledge and understanding of Place (AT2) — included to help teachers and teachers and pupils to identify key types of place covered in their teaching and learning.

Physical geography (AT3) — the shape and form of the landscape and the processes of the atmosphere, oceans and land (included to develop a branch of geography which was lacking in emphasis in recent years).

Human geography (AT4) — the social and economic

characteristics of the peoples who inhabit the earth and the processes by which changes in these occur.

Environmental geography (AT5) — include because of concern for the planet in the 1990s. Geography's role in environmental studies is a very large one.

B. Geographical terms

Absolute location — accurate description of location with reference to coordinates, grid references or to latitude and longitude.

Relative location — this is a sketch made outside or through the classroom window which records the main features in view. These features are normally grouped into physical features (shape of land etc.) and human features (how the land is used by humans), these are labelled on the sketch.

Primary industries — quarrying (mining), fishing, forestry, agriculture.

Secondary industries — those industries where the primary products and /or other secondary materials are manufactured into useable items.

Tertiary industries — chiefly service industries such as fire, police, health, education.

Quaternary industries — chiefly office based.

Oblique aerial photograph — the aerial photograph has been taken at an angle as oppose to a vertical view.

Geographical enquiry — this is and investigation which focuses upon a problem solving exercise or and issue of concern to the children and others. The enquiry consists of a sequence of questions carried out in a geographical context such as about a place or a thematic topic. So the children might carry out and enquiry into the best place for a school seat or the school traffic patrol. The Geographical Association in their leaflet *Implementing Geography in the National Curriculum, Key Stage, 1 and* 2, suggest the following.

— What is it?

— Where is it?

— What is it like?

- What is it about?
- How did it get like this?
- What physical and human processes caused it to be like this?
- How is the situation changing?
- What do people feel and think about this?

RESOURCES AND REFERENCES

What resources are necessary to teach geography in primary schools?

Since the introduction of the National Curriculum many schools feel inadequately resourced in geography. The geography coordinator first needs to look at what the schools already has and then list in order of priority those items which will be needed. We hope that the following list of items will help the geography coordinator to assess the resources needed. The list is neither prescriptive nor exhaustive in fact we have deliberately kept it short.

- Collection of maps: large scale maps of the local area and areas to be studied;
- Maps of the locality, region, the UK, Europe and the world (including projections other than the Mercator);
- Atlases and Globes. A-Z plans and shopping centre plans.
- Playmats;
- A wide selection of photographs, slides, films, television programmes depicting different people, buildings, places, landforms. these pictures need to reflect all aspects of geography;
- A selection of books on a variety of geographical topics for use with children. These could include the use of fiction as a starting point;
- A collection of measuring instruments; compasses, weather measuring instruments;
- Programmable toys such as *Roamer* or *Pip;*
- A collection of software including databases and

spreadsheets where children can store select and analyse information for themselves;

— A selection of photopacks for locality studies such as the Geographical Association's Focus on Castries, St. Lucia' pack;

— A collection of postcards, holiday memorabilia, rocks, fossils,

Useful books and publications for the staff library

DES *Geography 5-16, Curriculum Matters 7,* HMSO, London, 1986, Bale , J. *Geography in the Primary School,* Routledge and Keegan. Paul, London, 1987.

The Geographical Association has published several very useful publications such as *Place. A practical guide to teaching about places, 1992* and Mills, D. (Ed.) *Geographical work in Primary and Middle Schools,* 1987. The Geographical Association, 343 Fulwood Road, Sheffield, S10 3BP.

The magazine *Primary Geographer* also published by the GA is also very helpful.

It is worth getting your LEA or a group of schools together to approach local planning departments, local record offices or local newspaper offices to try to build up a pool of resources such as local plans, maps and aerial photographs. There are a number of companies that provide oblique, aerial and ground photographs, but these tend to be rather expensive.

Photopacks

The following addresses are useful for information about photopacks and further resources:

Action Aid, Hamlyn House, Archway, London, N19 5PG.

Development Education Dispatch Unit, 153 Cardigan Road, Leeds, LS6 1LJ.

Information technology

The most important contribution that IT can make to a geography curriculum is through the use of databases created to enhance the children's geographical work. For example information about the local area may be collected and entered into a database by one class of children, then another class could interrogate the existing data file. Similarly children could interrogate commercially produced data files. Programs which can enhance children's geographical experience, through adventure games, simulations and help in the revision and reinforcement of mapwork skills, are also available.

Twinning

More information on the 'twinning' scheme mentioned in this chapter can be found in *Cheshire Twinning* obtainable from the Langley Teacher's Centre Main Road, Langley, Macclesfield, Cheshire, SK11 0BU or Jeremy Krause, County Hall, Chester, CH1 1JQ.

Acknowledgements

The authors wish to thank Moreen Morron, David Farrell, Mavis Nixon, Linda Buxton and Sina Smith for their help in discussing the role of the geography coordinator.

They would also like to thank David Farrell and Karolyn Greenlees formerly of the Cheshire humanities Advisory Team, for permission to show the rolling planning programme that they developed for use in David's School.

BIBLIOGRAPHY

Bruner, J. *The Process of Education*, Random House, New York, 1963.

Greaves, N.J. and Naish, M. *Profiling in Geography,* Geographical Association, Sheffield, 1986.

Geographical Association. *Implementing Geography in the National Curriculum, Key Stages 1 and 2,* Geographical Association, Sheffield.

10

DESIGN TECHNOLOGY IN THE PRIMARY YEARS

INTRODUCTION

Some design technology coordinators may think that the challenges ahead are daunting.

— Class teachers may say that they lack the skills and the knowledge to meet the requirements of design technology.

— Resources my be scarce.

— Design technology seems to cover all areas of the curriculum.

— Headteachers and teaches often do not understand design technology.

— There is a mixed history of the subject in primary and in secondary schools.

— The goalposts keep moving.

In many ways the situation in the 90s for design technology matches that for science in the early 80s.

Many of the above points can be also used to work to the advantage of design technology coordinators. Your colleagues will look to you for leadership, they will be prepared to listen and they will want help.

Design technology for children demands active engagement. In this chapter we will examine how that same engagement will enable both teachers and children to move forward into high quality design technology experiences.

In my book, *Design Technology at Key Stages One and Two,* I have argued that whilst design technology is and essential subject in its own right, it might also be treated as a cross-curricular theme. This is one of its great strengths. Design technology as an active and broad area of experience can encompass and act as a catalyst for the whole curriculum for all children. *Entitlement* and *access* are key words when we consider design technology as part of every child's curriculum. Design technology should be flexible. At its best it is tailored to the needs of the children and those needs which they see in the world around them.

For themes will be developed to assist you:

1. The nature of design technology capability
2. The management of design technology
3. Developing an action plan as coordinator
4. Improving the qualify of design technology in your school.

This programmes an approach to design technology. This chapter will also lay out the meaning and the implications of the need. It will be important to clarify what we mean and what we want. For this purpose examples will be provided, alternatives examined, criteria considered, questions asked, and avenues of action explored and designed by the reader. We will move from our need towards the design of a solution. Concerns about the quality of experience involve an evaluation of provision judged against what a school considers to be good practice in that area.

THE NATURE OF DESIGN TECHNOLOGY CAPABILITY

The current definitions of design and technology have grown out of and historical base in craft subjects which often dealt with 'resistant materials'. The notion of craft was and remains very important. This area was traditionally referred to as CDT (Craft Design and Technology). Craft should now be balanced against other equally important aspects of design technology experience. The debate continues with some pressure to return to 'harder' technology such as electronics, particularly at Key Stages 3 and 4. When addressing these issues, we need to be clear about our aim, that is, to promote confidence, technological literacy and capability.

The vocabulary of design technology has been and still is a block to many teachers. As teachers grow in confidence however, this vocabulary will enable them to express ideas about children's capability in a way that was not possible previously. In primary education we have never had a professional vocabulary for design technology, in the way that we have for reading and mathematics for example. This does not, however, get over the initial reaction against 'jargon'. Indeed this was recognised as a significant difficulty in the report by HMI on the first year of implementation of the statutory orders for Technology.

Five Areas of Design Technology	*Divided into*	*Within the Topic of 'Homes'*
Programmes of Study	communication identification of needs artefacts, systems & environments materials	These headings help us to plan for breadth. What materials are used in furniture? Can we identify a need for a piece of furniture?
attainment targets	identifying needs & opportunities designing planning & making evaluating	Develop a series of design activities to do with furniture, electricity, materials, organisation etc.
outcomes	artefact system environment	An object made or used by humans i.e. pillow, cake. A heating system, a food rotation system. A room, a house, a play house.
context	home school community industry leisure	Our home, the homes of others, homes with school. How business and industry carter for homes.
	food	Designing and/or making foods.

materials	fabric constructional materials graphic media	Designing and making decorations. Communicating, design briefs or instructions.

Below is an activity which a group of teachers might carry out as they are becoming aware of the elements outlined above. You might ask colleagues to consider a recent topic or theme and to identify elements from any of the five areas we have just examined.

Five areas	*Divided into*	*In my topic/theme*
Programmes of Study	communicatior identification of needs artefacts, systems & environments materials	
attainment target	identifying needs & opportunities designing planning & making evaluating	
outcomes	artefact system environment	
contexts	home school community industry leisure	
materials	food fabric constructional materials graphic media	

You might like to repeat this activity in relation to a future theme or topic.

Presented in this way teachers can begin to see the very broad content and experiential base of design technology. This is a great strength in two expects:

— it allows access for teachers whose expertise lies in other areas, for example fabric or communication

— it means that cross-curricular links are more ready made.

A BALANCE OF PROCESS AND SKILS

A major debate has continued throughout the development of design technology. This has been about the emphasis on *skills* and on the so called *design process.* This debate continues and will no doubt appear and reappear as pressure groups and politicians seek to further influence the curriculum. What does not change is good quality design technology activity, which has gone on in primary schools for years often under the title of art or science or topic work. The national Curriculum statutory orders attempted to spell out what design technology is. However in their original form, there is considerable mismatch between the attainment targets (ATs) and the Programmes of Study (PoS).

Balance will need to be achieved across the attainment targets which, like AT 1 in science, are present in all design technology. It will be necessary therefore to focus your attention on an attainment target for a period of me whilst always being prepared to step back and look at the whole process.

In the 1991 APU report on children's performance in design technology, Chapter Two describes the early linear model of the design line:

DESIGN → MAKE → EVALUATE

and later the design cycle:

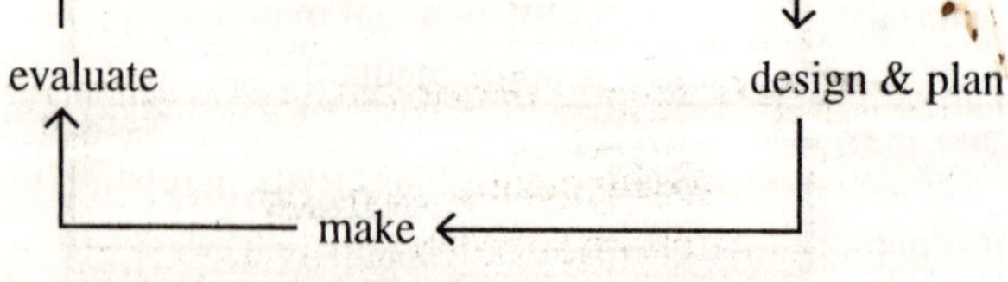

The cycle importantly include emphasis on identifying needs and on the role of evaluation. It is important that coordinators emphasise these as they are often neglected and require focus and attention in the classroom. The APU report goes on the describe some reservations with relation to both models and proposes a different model where design technology capability consists of both active and reflective capability.

This model is meaninging to many teachers as it describes what we see in the classroom. Children moving from action to thought and back again in a process which allows them to focus and refocus on the need and the outcome they have in mind. These models are presented here so that coordinators might give teachers a model around which to plan their teaching. Therefore it may be useful to examime with colleagues the limitations of earlier models and begin as a group to make your own interpretations.

It is questionable how far these models describe the complex process we see going on in the classroom. However, these models are useful as long as we accept their limitations and the fact that we cannot insist that children adhere to them. They are useful for planning in so far as they can act as an *aide-memoire* ensuring that we provide apprtunity for evaluation, planning and reflection.

As coordinator for Design Technology it will be essential for you to:

— exemplify good prectice through your own work;
— provide opportunities for colleagues to explore their under standing of key terms;
— show that design technology is already taught in the school but may not be recognised as such;
— reinforce the point thath all teachers have something to offer;
— show that basic literacy and numeracy can be developed through design technology activity;
— establish and persuade teachers of the streangth of taking a crosscurricular approach;
— help teachers to identify areas where they need to development in design technology;
— ensure continuity and progression in design technology, across and between year groups and within Key Stages,

by contributing ideas and suggestions during the planning of themes and topics.

A DESIGN TECHNOLOGY APPROACH TO DESIGN TECHNOLOGY!

It will be useful to adopt a design technology approach to your own development and to that of your colleagues and the school. Just as a food technologist might design a series of healthy meals for a group of children going camping, we have to design a diet of activities which we call a programme of study. Furthermore, remember that evaluation is as important to the design technologist as it is to the teacher. Action, review and reflection is a useful model for both teaching and design technology.

Six key points to be communicated by the design technology coordinator

1. Design technology requires children to be active and engaged.
2. Design technology contexts are motivating for young children and that motivation needs to be harnessed.
3. Design technology is essentially cross-curricular.
4. Design technology is best developed from a meaningful context.
5. Breadth, balance and progression are all important.
6. Design technology can enrich or be enriched by any other curricula areas yet can exist discretely, and a good strategy over a year is to balance these approaches.

THE MANAGEMENT OF DESIGN TECHNOLOGY

Schools need to have:

— clearly stated aims which are exemplified in a policy document;

— a member of staff with developing expertise to act as a consultant and in some cases a specialist;

— and INSET programme which allows all teachers to improve their technological capacity;

- a planning strategy which allows design technology to be built into the curriculum so that
  - sufficient time is devoted to it
  - breadth and balance are achieved
  - continuity and progression are achieved
- a system of record keeping;
- sufficient accommodation and resources;
- periodic review by individual teachers, by the coordinator, by the headteacher, by the whole staff.

Management at school level

The school's policy should address all of the above managerial prerequisites and include the requirements of the National Curriculum. It should make clear, unambiguous statements with examples so that the terminology does not confuse teachers. It might briefly:

- make a statement of intent; perhaps a separate short statement of policy;
- be clear about the necessity for good quality, balanced and relevant design technology; exemplify its cross-curricular nature;
- state the learning outcomes which might be expected so that teachers establish a rationale for design technology;
- describe how the planning of the whole-school curriculum affects design technology in that plans for all the foundation subjects will have implications for design technology;
- describe the record keeping system for design technology;
- give advice on;
  - achieving breadth, balance, continuity and progression
  - differentiating for ability groups
  - assessing children's progress
  - ideas for content and say where these might be found

  - appropriate materials
  - the use of tools and safety
  - addressing gender issues
  - ensuring reference to and full use of cultural and ethnic diversity;
- give information about:
  - the resources available for design technology in school and procedures for ordering additional items
  - local advisory support
  - courses
  - transition across phases.

The policy may also include the coordinator's job description. It should be seen as a focus for continuing development in the school and not as a once-and-for-all statement consigned to the headteacher's filing cabinet awaiting the next school inspection. A good test of a policy document is to ask a recently appointed teacher how much use it was! Furthermore do remember to re-read in yourself as you review design technology in the classroom or across one or two Key Stages.

Planning

Planning strategies for the whole-school must allow for design technology to be implemented fully in each Key Stage. A common strategy as a basis for planning is outlined below.

Key Stage 1 Each topic will include the three core subjects to some degree along with art and movement. Selected foundation areas are rotated to ensure breadth and balance. Schools might adapt this by removing or adding foundation subjects from the rotation. There is little scope for rotating the core areas, but enormous scope for linking them with the below.

Term 1		*Term 2*		*Term 3*	
a	*b*	*a*	*b*	*a*	*b*
		Year 1			
Ourselves	Festivals	Changes	Spring	Water	Holidays
d.& t. music	history geog. music	d.& t. history	geog. music	geog. history d. & t.	music geog. d. & t.
		Year 2			
Animals	Then and now	Food	Our Locality	Machines	Castles
geog. music	music d. & t. history	geog. d.& t. history	geog. history	d. & t. music	music d. & t. history

Examples of planning for balance across foundation subjects at Key Stage 1

Design technology does not have to be happening all the time. You will have to consider together whether the plan suggested above is sufficient (four design technology foci per year), as well as what you mean by a focus. Are these times when a topic will be totally design technology and others where design technology is a significant element? Balance is achieved by teachers who are well informed about what has gone on and who understand the subject and the plans for the Key Stage.

Elements from contexts, outcomes and materials might be allocated to topics. For example in the plan for term 3, year two's theme is Castles. In design technology we might emphasise: *history:* material — food (researching and making medieval food). *music:* context — homes (comparison then and now — kitchens), *design & technology:* outcomes — environment (construct from plan).

This will not mean that the teacher is limited to these elements, rather that the teacher is asked to focus on these and to ensure coverage. The teacher is, of course, likely to deal with more than just food as a material in this topic.

Alternatives exist, one is to plan or promote short sub topics which would allow teachers over a shorter term, (say a few days to a couple of weeks) to address elements of design technology.

CONTINUITY — THE FIRST ESSENTIAL?

Progression cannot be usefully addressed before continuity of experience is assured. This can only be achieved by teachers who have developed a good understanding of what design technology is and how they are going to approach it with their classes.

At one level continuality is fairly straightforward and can be achieved by and agreed school-wide consistency in teachers':

— approach to processes in design technology;

— use of and range of materials;

— constraints on contexts, materials, tools;

— policy on the use of tools and children's safety;

— use of discussion and questioning;

— approach to recording (of activity by the children).

At another level it is more demanding;

— What constitutes progress and how will we record it?

— What forms of assessment will we use?

— Do we have a shared understanding of the assessment criteria?

— How do we use the information gained during assessment?

When a number of these are achieved we can start to come to terms with progression. It is tied up with differentiation, assessment playing a key role. Progression is also dealt with under the title 'Developing Quality in Design Technology', later in this chapter.

DEVELOPING AN ACTION PLAN AS COORDINATOR

Your action plan will need to account for:

— the notion of entitlement for all;

— where the school is and where you and the staff want to be;

— particulars of the school and its children;

— the mix of capabilities amongst the teachers and their needs;

— development of other areas within the school;

— the demands of statutory orders, assessment and recording;

— the need to communicate with all involved, primarily parents and other teachers.

Establishing goals

It is worth writing down *all* the things you wish to achieve. Then identify six to ten of the most significant. Divide these into those which look possible and those which look more difficult.

You might use these listings to establish an order of priority:

Short- term goals (one year) long-term goals (three-five years).

This will help you establish your overall aims which will be achieved by progress towards these goals or objectives. To address these goals successfully they will need to be the focus of your attention. This is a good point to talk everything through with the headteacher, so that your thinking is in line with more general development plans for the school. This dialogue with head must be maintained.

Your short-term goals (three to five for a year) might include:

— holding a staff meeting;

— making decisions about planning;

— clarifying the nature of design and technology;

— establishing a resource base including essential items.

You will need to pace yourself on these over the year ahead so that you do not have everything to do in the last term.

Your longer term goals will need to be addressed at the same time. Here you may be concerned to:

— develop a design technology policy statement and policy document of file;

— establish an improved resource provision, including the need for consumables;

— develop record keeping in design technology;

— inform parents.

The last two items may be first attempted in your own class. It will also allow you to say that *you* have done it! Item one above to be addressed in the first year, perhaps with a one page statement of policy and an early draft of other material.

Your own personal professional development

An essential element in your plan of action will be your own personal professional development. This should be planned and tied into the school's appraisal scheme. As your agenda emerges its execution needs to be reviewed annually, perhaps as part of a school appraisal scheme or personally after a period of evaluation and reflection.

Find out about or introduce yourself to:

— local courses; local advisors or advisory teachers;
— the Design and Technology Association;
— the Association of Science Education;
— your local SEMERC and SATRO;
— another design technology coordinator in a neighbouring primary school;
— your local secondary school design technology department.

Make yourself aware of:

— national and local initiatives;
— SCAA publications;
— publishers' materials.

Your own professional development in one year might include the following aims to:

— become aware of publications, and read a selection of reports;
— collect articles and useful addresses;
— negotiate a job description for yourself with your headteacher;
— attend a short course;
— devise your plan of action and carry it out;
— enlist your school in the Design and Technology Association (DATA);

— identify a longer course for the future and possibly consider same action research;

— develop your own classroom practice as a teacher of technology;

— meet the Head of Technology in your local high school;

— evaluate this year and plan for the next.

All requires considerable effort, so be realistic. If any of the above lists look confersing select from within them. Remember, you can do a lot in one year if you start early. Finally remember one reason for an action plan is to so identify the things that you have *not* been able to do so that you can include them later on. Try to enjoy it. If you can, you have every chance of success. If, however, the tasks you user yourself are too many and so onerous, your are unlikely to convince others!

DEVELOPING QUALITY IN DESIGN TECHNOLOGY

Consideration of quality involves us in reflection and evaluation as part of a design situation. Have we designed and implemented a curriculum of quality? Quality in provision for design technology can be achieved by giving particular attention to the following aspects of your work, which can then be regarded as performance indicators:

— the extent of differentiated work for individual needs;

— the active nature of design technology;

— progression;

— children's involvement;

— access for all;

— record keeping;

— breadth;

— assessment;

— the product;

— cross-curricular links.

These cannot all be dealt with individually here, therefore a selection are outlined briefly and references are provided so that you may consider them in greater depth.

Differentiation

Differentiation requires that teachers know the children's level of attainment, what is to be achieved in design technology, how to implement it effectively, and something of how children learn.

1. Differentiation by task:

Here the teacher provides different activities in order to cater for individuals and /or groups. Knowledge of children's attainment has to be accurate as does the teacher's judgement. For example, in the construction of a helmet quite different instructions will be given: open ended for one group and step by step instructions for another.

2. Differentiation by outcome:

Here open ended tasks are presented to the whole group. The various group and individual responses will establish differentiation. The teacher needs to be aware of possible differences between children teacher and allow them to respond to the task differently. In this case one simple set of instructions is given with the aim of stimulating varying attainments.

Key areas for consideration are:

- What do we mean by differentiation?
- What is the teacher's role?
- What teaching styles are available and appropriate?
- What are the children's learning styles?
- Preferred and effective organisational strategies;
- The required depth in planning that is necessary;
- The content and the process of design technology.

Differentiation can mean well matched activities for youngsters, but it must not become limiting, to the extent that teachers prejudge groups and individuals, denying children the opportunity to demonstrate capability. We should consider employing both differentiation by task and differentiation by outcome. It will be a useful strategy to balance the use of these so that one avoids the disadvantages of each.

Progression

In *Curriculum Organisation and Classrom Practice in Primary*

Schools progression is identified by Alexander, Rose and Woodhead as being the 'touchstone for all decisions about teaching' (paragraph 128).

Progression is undoubtedly significant in design technology. You may find that where teachers start design technology in the classroom, they may have difficulty deciding the next steps when a task is complete or a skill mastered. Often this can be related to the fact that many teachers have not experienced this progression personally.

You may find that progression is best tackled after teachers have begun to understand more of the subject and to use design technology in their planning following an INSET course.

A number of approaches exist:

1. Consider existing areas of progression which teachers seem to understand, such as

   — progression in the use of simple tools

   — progression in learning to tell the time.

   Consider for example, progression in the use of scissors: tearing and separating; snipping; cutting out pictures; cutting a range of materials; cutting around a shape; making choices about materials; cutting out a shape; choosing an appropriate cutting tool (more detail in Cross 1993).

   From this, teachers can move on to understand progression in less well known capabilities in design technology such as drilling, designing and evaluating.

2. Consider a common design technology situation such as, designing a playground; designing a meal or designing a play environment in a cafe. How might children in the early years approach it?

   What about children in years three-five?

   What might we be aiming for with children who are successful in this early experience?

3. Examine the five areas of design technology: the Programmes of Study, attainment targets, outcomes, contexts and materials which were listed earlier. These all have potential for progression. Choose one area together

and, as a staff, decide what it means. Consider where the children will start, particularly those who have had very little design technology experience, and where you might wish to take them.

4. Consider the aims of design technology (as stated in your policy document) and your aims with regard to the five areas above and their associated listed earlier. It is important to know why we are doing something. A good example is reading. Most teachers know why they are developing it and the main features involved in children's progression in reading. This is not always true for design technology!

5. If you have children's records for design technology which span part of a Key Stage, select one or two for examination by colleagues and consider whether progression is discernable.

The above are foci for attention, debate and discussion. Your colleagues will need this if they have not done it before in design technology. This will be useful after any significant staff changes and periodically, as a focus for review.

Assessment and record keeping

It is not possible to say which of these comes first in design technology. As a school, teachers need to develop them together. It is perhaps useful to start by considering the questions:

- What will I need to know?
- What will parents want to know?
- What will be useful for the next teacher to know?
- How will children, teachers and parents be involved?

This will focus your attention on the information and evidence you wish to record. Other questions will include:

- What informations available?
- How will we collect this information?
- What role might the children have in assessment and record keeping? Do we as team understand the statements of attainment (SoAs)?

— How will we present our assessment in a summative form?

— How will we communicate the results of assessment to parents?

Interim Record for Design Technology

class__________date__________theme__________

focus of assessment____________________

(SoAs)__________________________

criteria	names							
holistic view other elements of this AT? other ATs?								

An interim record for Design Technology (from Cross 1993)

Teachers will require help to interpret SoAs. They will need to consider evidence, its amount, its nature and how much and where to store it and record it. It is essential that you as a staff treat this as a learning process.

Access to design technology for all

— **Misunderstanding** by their teacher of either the subject or their abilities;

— The choice or **context** might display some **girls** or ethnic groups, for example, by constant reference to certain leisure activities;

— The use of certain **materials;**

— Presentation of **tasks.** Boys found difficulty dealing with open ended situations (APU, 1992);

— Use of **language;**

— Ignorance of or inability to cater for a child's **specific needs** (sensory, motor, cognitive, emotional, behavioural)

The first point has received attention earlier and so we will examine the others briefly. As coordinator it is your responsibility to be involved where a child may be denied access to design technology.

Choice of context

There has been an attempt to deal with this in the Non-Statutory Guidance which sets out five headings of contexts to be addressed:

home

school

recreation

community

business and industry.

Rather than attempt to apply such advice to the letter, we should use it as a guide and aim to achieve its spirit. This represents a significant challenge in many classrooms. Experiences in each of these areas so varied and different groups in the class will be likely to influence the teacher in how aspects of a theme are dealt with. The criteria must be:

— what will interest the children?

— what will allow development of the capabilities needed?

— how does this contribute to balance?

There will need to be balance over the year, which will become apparent as each term progresses. Often there is a group of younger children whose needs and interests may be quite different from the rest. Many teacher find it generally useful to select open ended themes such as our food, toys and games, rather than very specific topics, thus giving more flexibility.

Use of materials

We must increase our experience of materials so that we can offer a range to children. This has resourcing and storage implications. Variety is an important part of design technology experience. We should avoid using the same materials week out. Ideally we should give choice and aim for a time when children can choose materials based on previous experience or can plan a simple evaluation of new materials.

Presentation of tasks

APU research discovered that in a large sample, the results of gender groups were predictable according to the type of tasks presented. Girls performed better than boys in open ended, reflective tasks. In closed tasks the girls performed less well, particularly and significantly those girls identified as being of lower ability. From this evidence there are lessons to be learnt about:

— girls and boys working cooperatively in both mixed and single sex groups;
— individual strengths, weaknesses and under achievement;
— teachers' understanding of the nature of design technology tasks
— the need provide a mixture of both open and closed tasks;
— differentiation as a high priority;
— paying particular attention to vulnerable groups.

Use of language

Take care with the use of language at all times, and especially when dealing with technological terms.

Of course, we must remember that a child can use vocabulary to good effect but it is less that the sum of words known. This is well known to experienced teachers, but it does not stop many of us falling into the trap from time to time.

Language as a form of communication and a medium for investigation is essential to design technology. Design technology presents a powerful medium for the development of language.

Individual needs

There may be a fifth of children in every class with learning needs which affect their performance. A smaller proportion have needs so specific that they may require a statement which will indicate how access to the curriculum should be guaranteed. It must be remembered that some of these children may be particularly able and that all of them have more abilities than disabilities. The first group will generally be dealt with by use of strategies outlined here and in the rest of the book. Well planned teaching is the greatest ally to these children.

Other children require:

- an individual programme;
- space;
- adapted or particular tools;
- particular resources or materials;
- a high level of adult support.

Generally all children are motivated by similar things. Resources are important. If, for example, only traditional junior hacksaws are available, then grip will be difficult for some children. Work surfaces can present difficulties to children who have problems with mobility or motor control. Facilities to clamp work to a bench may need to be very flexible. The emphasis should be in what the children can do and what the individual child might progress towards.

Developing quality in design technology : the role of the coordinator

This is the heart of the matter. Teachers have consistently admitted to a lack of confidence in design technology. However it is part of every child's curriculum entitlement. In order to avoid lip service and mediocre design technology clear leadership is necessary. This requires that coordinators:

- start from what the teachers know and can teach;
- encourage colleagues;
- focus colleagues' attention on various aspects of the subject in order to make progress;
- provide a high level of leadership;

— are clear about what is meant by good design technology;
— determine performance indicators;
— encourage reflection and evaluation.

CONCLUSION

The product

What is the product of a Key Stage in design technology?

You should communicate to colleagues your vision of what the end product ought to be. Is it to do with the products which the children make? Is it to so with the experience and capability gained? Is it to do with boxes filled on a chart? Is it to do with the perception of parents about what their child is doing?

The answer has to do with all of these things and more. It is essential to state your intention clearly in a school policy and in your development plan. Design technology requires time for implementation and some colleagues may need persuasion, particularly if classroom management is affected. It may be wise to aim for small changes, encourage them and be encouraged by them. This approach will allow you to deal with the bigger issues in the long term.

BIBLIOGRAPHY

ASE Technology. *Policy Statement,* ASE, Hatfield, 1991.

Binden, A. and Cole, P. *Teaching Design & Technology,* Blackie, London, 1991.

Cross, A. *Designing a Place in the Curriculum, Design and Technology Teaching,* Vol. 24, No. 2., pp 22-24, 1992.

Chadwick, E. *Collins Primary Technology for Key Stage One-Teacher's Guide,* Collins, London, 1990.

Department of Education and Science and the Welsh Office. *Technology in the national Curriculum,* HMSO, London 1990.

Department of Education and Science. *Aspects of Primary Education: The Teaching and Learning of Design Technology,* HMSO, London, 1991.

Department of Education and Science. *Technology Key Stages 1,*

2 and 3 : A Report by H M I on the First Year, 1990-91, HMSO, London, 1992.

The Design Council Primary Education Working Party. *Design and Primary Education,* The Design Council, London, 1987.

Eggleston, J. *Teaching Design and Technology*, Open University Press, Buckingham.

Idle, 1. *Hands-on Technology,* Stanley Thornes, London, 1991.

Johnsey. R *Design and Technology through Problem Solving,* Simon and Schuster, London, 1990.

Lever, C. *National Curriculum Design Technology for Key Stages 1, 2 and 3,* Trentham Books, Stoke-on-Trent, 1990.

Somerset LEA. *Primary Design Technology Guidelines,* Somerset County Council, 1990.

Mount, M., and Ackerman , D. *Technology For All,* Fulton, London, 1991.

Williams, P. and Jinks. D. *Design and Technology 5-12,* Falmer London, 1985.

Williams, P. *Teaching Craft Design and Technology five to Thirteen,* Routledge, London, 1990.

USEFUL ADDRESS

DATA (Design and Technology Ass.), 16 Wellesbourne House, Warwickshire. Tel: 0789 470007 Fax: 0789 841955. National Subject Association, individuals and schools may join. Regional groups being established.

Economatics (Education) Ltd., Epic House, 18-20 Darnell Road, Attercliffe, Sheffield S9 5AA., Tel: 0742 561122.

A growing primary science and technology catalogue,

Heron Educational Ltd., Unit 3, Carrwood House, Carrwood Road, Sheepbridge, Chesterfield, S41 9QB. Tel: 0246 453354.

A growing primary science and technology catalogue suppliers of the Techtruck.

Leo (UK) Ltd., Ruthin Rd., Wrexham, Clywd. Tel: 0978 290900.

A wide range of construction kits, teacher material and spares available from this address.

Longman Logotron Ltd., Dales Brewery, Gwydir Street, Cambridge, CB 1 2LJ. Tel: 0223 323656.

A wide range of primary software, including Pendown, Revelation, Pinpoint.

NCET, sir William Lyons Rd., Science Park, Coventry, CV4 7EZ.

11
COMPUTERS IN THE CURRICULUM

Ten years ago teachers who used television programmes and occasionally employed a tape recorder were considered to be using advanced teaching technology. Now with the explosion of IT equipment into schools, teachers can incorporate the use of computers, modems, scanners, light and temperature sensors, floor robots and CD-Roms into children's everyday work. But do they? This chapter is designed to give heart to IT coordinators fighting on uphill battle on behalf of primary children. Amongst other themes it gives practical guidance on organising resources, supporting the curriculum and motivating staff - just three of the roles of the IT coordinator.

HMI report pioneer classes where micros augment work of every kind. LEAs produce curriculum guidelines with hosts of examples of working IT innovation. Individual schools feature on TV and their confident and articulate computer-literate children extol the virtues of the techniques which they have mastered for handling information. The only requirement of you, as IT coordinators is simply to manage a system where resources follow need and vibrant, enthusiastic teachers reach out for every opportunity to enhance children's experience with information technology. You can sit back and reap the benefit of praise for a job well done.

If you are thinking 'This doesn't sound like me!' - take heart. The reality for most IT coordinators is very different. In 1989 a Micro Educational Support Unit (MESU) report commented:

'There remains a wide gulf between what inspired things can be done with computers in primary schools and the limited way in which the technology is used by some teachers'.

The result of an ESRC research project in 1988 into the use of IT in primary schools in Scotland reported considerable scepticism amongst teachers.

'...it has been assumed that the benefits will be self evident to teachers' (this was not so)... 'less than half the forty teachers ... through there was a general positive effect from their use'.

I recently organised a survey of computer use in 1022 schools in one metropolitan area to see if this had changed. It showed that around a third of computers (29%) were not even switched on at the time of the survey, and many others were being used for fairly trivial matters. Furthermore these results came only from the 270 most interested schools of my sample — those who had taken the time and effort to find out how their computers were being used and to fill in my questionnaire. If you are in such a situation, this chapter is particularly for you. You are not alone. The typical IT coordinator carries this responsibility alongside at least one other curricular area and carries a full time teaching commitment. The IT coordinator is expected to be a technical wizard, a software consultant, know everyone's curricular needs and be able to do all this with little or no resources — and always by yesterday.

By reading this chapter, alongside Chapter One, you should be able to find useful ideas in order to become more effective in your role, gain some satisfaction from attaining a number of your goals and serve the interests of children throughout your school by achieving an improvement in their IT experience.

The role of the curriculum coordinator in your school will be peculiar to its history, the strengths of other staff, the interests of the headteacher and the way in which you assume responsibility. The current desire for watertight job specifications can militate against you developing a role which grows with your experience and confidence in this area. At all times you will need to reach agreement with your headteacher as to the boundaries and priorities for your actions. Each of the school's curriculum coordinators needs to consider the ways in which computers may be used in their particular subject areas. It is your task to help them and this can be achieved in a number of ways:

— Work with colleagues in order to develop a commonly understood policy.

— Provide some technical support.
— Maintain an overview of the use of computers throughout the school.
— Help teachers to see where work in IT can support teaching and learning.
— Provide colleagues with guidance in assessing children's attainment in IT.
— Organise resources so that they are accessible.
— Act as a link with outside agencies.
— Support and encourage colleagues.

TECHNICIAN OR TEACHER?

The coordinator for PE has a responsibility to see that the apparatus has a regular safety check, the Maths coordinator possibly looks after the balances. They are not expected to mend them! However if your experience is typical then you can fill your school hours responding to requests for technical assistance. More than one coordinator has been asked to leave his or her class to see to a computer, connect a turtle, solve a disc problem. What do *you* do?

One IT coordinator was sent a note first thing on Monday morning. This urgently requested that she leave her classroom to come and switch on another teacher's computer in a different part of the building as it was needed in that lesson. On her arrival the class teacher told her that all weekend water had dripped into the machine from a leaky roof. As it might be dangerous the class teacher through it would be better if the coordinator switched it on!

Most coordinators send back a polite, helpful message back but refuse to leave their children unattended. Normal lesson preparation includes making sure that the equipment needed — be it paper, paint, PE apparatus or floor turtles — are present and in working order. Teachers may need encouragement to think well in advance in order that when you may be needed for consultation and even emergency action you will be free to give assistance.

Keep a record over the next month of the technical matters about which you have been consulted. What times of the day did they occur, was the solution in the hands of the teacher or did it really need your expertise, how can teachers avoid getting into such difficulties in the future? From this record you may be able to set up a training activity, or define a maintenance contract/schedule which will cut down the frequency of the need for your presence.

There is, of course, a case for having someone on the staff who has taken the time and trouble to learn to cope with some of the technical matters which can get in the way of computers efficiently. That someone is you. In order to encourage teachers to take computers home, for example, you will need to show them what function is played by each part of the system and how the various components are interconnected. When repairs are needed, you may need to understand and describe something of the malfunction and put the system back together on its return to school. Manuals and guidebooks should be read and important matters highlighted, so that the attention of other readers will be attached to essential information.

I draw the line whenever a screwdriver is needed. Unless you are familiar with the maintenance of electronic devices, leave anything which involves tools and dismantling parts of the machine to those paid to deal with such things. If any accident should occur as a result of your untrained experimentation inside a machine, it will be no-one's fact but your own.

Certain preventative measures can be taken to minimise the breakdowns which happen in schools. Teachers need to be persuaded to exit from program properly. It is not uncommon for a teacher to unplug the micro whist the programme is still running; the teacher then complains of continual disc errors.

Care of discs in general can save you a lot of problems. Of course accidents will happen, but if you can find way to minimise them it will make your life easier.

Some coordinators have trained one or two children from each class to help preserve discs from the most common abuses. Their main job is to ensure that discs are removed from computers before they are switched off. Discs do not like to be left on top of radiators, put close to the monitor, bent, written upon or made wet. Children need to be taught that the shiny part, which is the magnetic media, is particularly susceptible to sticky fingers and should be protected by keeping the disc in its envelope whenever possible. Children are your best allies in the crusade against disc errors.

Organising software

The first expectation of class is that their IT coordinator should know all about the software packages currently in school. If you are new to the post will need to build up a knowledge of the school's stock of programs. This can be done by collating information already available on regularly used programs. A simple index box will suit your purpose. Jot down everything you hear teachers say about sundry software packages and have this information to hand when asked to advise. You will no doubt transfer this information to a suitable database at a later date. This also applies to items you would like to buy.

If relatively new to IT preserver with using software to keep your own records. It will eventually save you time and effort and impress and influence your colleagues.

However, the pile of unmarked discs and lost manuals separated from their discs will cause any newcomer to the job to despair in the first few weeks.

Do not panic

If the school has been able to manage with such chaos over a number of years then a few more months will not hurt.

Enlist the help of any sympathetic teachers to find out just what you do have.

Buy some freezer labels and stick them on each disc.

Distribute two or three discs at a time to your colleagues and ask them to write on the labels in felt pen (biros will damage the discs). Negotiate a deadline for each task or you may be hindered rather than helped. In this way you will start to make sense of the multiple versions, damaged discs and pirate copies which, no doubt, will be present in the pile.

Destroy any copyright materials which you suspect to be pirate copies. You do not want the first money you obtain to go on the payment of fines for breach of copyright.

Attempt to match the discs with their booklets.

The accompanying documentation which publishers supply with their software will vary in quality, quantity and type. It is a rare booklet that is of no use to anyone — unless it is separated from its disc, of course. You should ensure that packages returned to you still have the documentation.

Keep a record of what you have found.

Use your index file. You will then be on your way to organising the resources so that they will be useful to people. At first you may wish just to record these and catalogue them alphabetically. This may from the basis of your first newsletter to staff. Later as you grow to understand the teachers' needs in your school and have had a chance to see some of the software in action in classrooms you may choose to catalogue them in terms of age-suitability or give copies to appropriate classes.

Some of the discs you find will be master copies. These should not be used by the children. Make backup copies of these and lack away the original securely. Be assured that the first time you decide that it will not matter if you use the master copy for once — it will!

The organisation of access to software is a perennial problem for coordinators. You may come up with ingenious solutions but mainly you have three basic choices:

1. Keep discs and associated documentation centrally. Give a copy of the list of programs to each teacher. When any class teacher wants to use a particular disc, book it out to them. Keep backup copies in a separate place in order to take account for accidental damage to discs.
2. Make multiple copies of popular programs so that each teacher can have their own. You will also need to consider whether to make copies of the handbook where allowed.
3. Issue discs to the most suitable class or department, keeping a note of who has what. The locations of the discs will have to be issued to all teachers by means of a general list. Make frequent checks of the discs and documentation. **Remember, never give anyone a master disc.**

The system you choose will need to account for the types of

computer in your school, the convenience of a location for central licence or single copy software. What is most important however is the quality of information teachers have about the available software.

Teachers need simple tabulated information detailing the name of the program, its purpose (word processing, art package, database, adventure program) and the age range for which it has been designed and tried out. This will help teachers to make choices. They also need to have to hand, information on how the program works, examples of how it has been used before, what away-from-the-compute work is associated with the package, any special features or accessories needed and how to print out finished work.

Hopefully you will purchase software which includes much of this information in the accompanying documentation. It will prove a worthwhile investment to buy folders for each of your main programs. Put both the disc and booklet in the folder with examples of use by teachers in your school. Clear plastic foolscap folders with zip openings are best for this job in order that the contents are visible. The graphs children have drawn thing data handling packages, fancy lettering used in stories children might have written, a teacher's jotting on the work children did as are result of adventure program, are all examples of items teachers would find useful in such envelopes. Example of an information sheet for junior Pinpoint:

This database package for the A3000 consists of one disc and an accompanying children's booklet. The booklet has been designed to introduce children to the concept of database as well as this programme. It also contains example files. Suitable for Yr 3, 4, 5, 6.

Additional Contents: Comment by Mr. Timms on use by Yr 4 Summer 1992. 3-D Pie Char used by head to show budget share - Spring 1993.

This is merely an extension of the 'pooling' of topic worksheets which goes on in many schools. By creating browsable packages you may make a contribution to a change in some teachers' use of IT.

One coordinator commented: 'I printed a children's instruction for LOCO on one side of A4 and suggested that teachers pinned it up on the wall beside the computer so that children have a constant reference. This had helped the acceptance of work in this area. In fact the other day I found two members of staff using the sheet to learn about LOGO themselves. They stopped of course, as soon as I came near'.

SUPPORTING THE CURRICULUM THROUGH IT AND SUPPORTING THE IT CURRICULUM

Your task in this area is to examine the work going on your colleagues' classrooms. See whether you can make helpful suggestions to encourage them to support their children's learning through work in IT wherever sensible. A good knowledge of the requirements of the National Curriculum Programmes of Study in each area should help you to determine where approaches might be welcomed. The Non-Statutory Guidance for Technology identifies five strands of IT capability:

1. Developing ideas and communicating information
2. Handling information
3. Modelling
4. Measurement and control
5. Applications and effects.

Software associated with communicating information:

All about me; Caption; Folio; Airbrush; Concept Writer, WRITE; Front Page Extra; More about me; Ease; Phases; Draw; Paint; Pendown; Revelation; Intro Tray; Compose, Notate.

Software associated with handling information:

Datashow; Graph it; Chatwell; Sorting Game; All about us; Branch; Junior PinPoint; Animal Pack; Datacalc; Datafind; List explorer; Datashow.

Software associated with modelling:

Moving in; Our school; My world; Landmarks; Granny's Garden; Mallory Towers; Craftshop; Jumbo; Toy Cupboard; Elmtree Farm.

Software associated with measurement and control:

Dart; Logotron LOGO; Crash; Screen Turtle; Mazes and robotic toys such as Big Trak, PIP, Roamer.

Teachers will be unfamiliar with some stands of IT capability but can be led gently into considering each aspect by relating it to their

National Curriculum subject levels	*Design Technology*					*English*					*Mathematics*						*Science*				
	1	*2*	*3*	*4*	*5*	*1*	*2*	*3*	*4*	*5*	*1*	*2*	*3*	*4*	*5*	*6*	*1*	*2*	*3*	*4*	*5*
DATABASES																					
Enter data			■	■				□	□	□			■		■			■	■	■	■
Retrieve data			■			■	■	■	■	■			■	■	■	■	■	■	■	■	■
Identify appropriate uses				□														□			
Create a database			□		■			□	□	□		□						□			
WORD PROCESSING																					
Manipulate text			□		□	■	■	■	■	■								□	□	□	□
Present information	□	□	■	■	■	■	■	■	■	■				□		□		□	□	□	□
SPREADSHEETS																					
Retrieve data			□	□	□											■			□	■	■
Create a spreadsheet			□															□		■	■

■ It use *explicitly* mentioned in the National Curriculum Attainment Targets

□ It use *appropriate* to the Attainment Targets.

current work. Communicating through manipulating text in a variety of ways for a variety of purpose will lead to discussion of the rival merits of word processing packages, for example. Modelling is best exemplified by the plans children have made on paper to find Tom and his friends in *Granny's Garden.*

However, it will be by reference to standard packages — databases, word processing, that teachers are most likely to see the links with other areas of the curriculum. This chart has been worked out using data from NCET. It shows the advantage of using purposeful and directed computer work, integrated into every class. With this chart you will be able to advise on the types of software available and the uses to which these programs may be put.

What's happening in other schools?

The survey referred to earlier asked teachers about the use to which their class computer was being put at one specified time in a week in January.

Word processing

Word processing is the most popular single use of computers in primary schools. It can help children to become familiar with the keyboard in the Initial phase, it removes the need for simultaneous concentration on all the aspects of production and encourages drafting, checking for errors, editing and collaborative writing in later stages.

The use of different fonts and borders simulates a sense of audience and the final product can usually be produced in a number of formats — large such as for the wall display, medium size to accompany a picture, small for an early in a newspaper or collection of works. A variety of word processing packages with different facilities is needed to help children to write for various audiences. For example children may want to write:

- newspaper reports;
- an obituary;
- a play script;
- the musings of a famous person;
- a school report;

— evidence from a trial;
— a short story;
— an advertisement for the paper;
— a conversation;
— instructions (recipe or directions);
— a 17th century version of a modern tale;
— a message in a bottle;
— a doctor's report;
— a poster;
— a letter/postcard to a friend;
— a job application;
— a latter of complaint.

<table>
<tr><th>N'Sery</th><th>Recep'n</th><th>Yr1</th><th>Yr2</th><th>Yr3</th><th>Yr4</th><th>Yr5</th><th>Yr6</th></tr>
<tr><td colspan="3">BBC</td><td colspan="5">A3000</td></tr>
<tr><td colspan="2">Folio with Concept Keyboard</td><td>Folio</td><td colspan="3">Phases</td><td colspan="2">Desktop Folio</td></tr>
<tr><td colspan="2">No database work currently planned</td><td>Our Facts</td><td colspan="3">Datasweet</td><td colspan="2">Junior Pinpoint</td></tr>
<tr><td colspan="4">Roamer</td><td colspan="2">Floor T'tle</td><td colspan="2">LOGOTRON LOGO</td></tr>
</table>

One school coordinator gained agreement for a whole-school policy in the use of some applications with continuity and progression in mind.

They might find using only one type of word processing package quite limiting. One the other hand it might be desirable to persuade teachers to follow a whole-school policy in this area to ensure continuity and progression.

Databases

Databases are frequently used to show children (and adults) the power of the computer. The speed at which micros can make calculations, sort data, and the graphic capabilities employed to show the results, are all impressive. The instances of children using them, however, are less frequent. These are two ways in which teachers choose to introduce children to work with databases.

Children and Databases - Method 1

Imagine introducing children to a new concept: books. We would show them a variety of books, picture books, textbooks, books in foreign languages, books for infants, scientific books, storybooks and so on. After some familiarisation you might suggest that children make their own books based closely on one or more of the example. We should approach the introduction of databases in the same way.

Children and Database - Method 2

The best way to introduce children to the idea of a database is to make one as a response to children's own needs. A sensitive teacher will arrange a project or simulate a problem to arise from children's own work where the solution lies in the creation and use of a database.

Whichever package you choose, you will be able to obtain specimen files. Use these at home. Find out what analyses are possible. How can you print out a list or a pie chart? Can you readily delete or replace a file? Can you print out individual records? Can you analyse a subset of data only? Do the publishers suggest ways in which your class could use the program?

Drill and practice

These programs are often scathingly attacked as the unacceptable face of computer use. You might argue however, that such programs often support specific learning objectives, generally give instant reward, appeal to some students the work can allow for differentiation (the rest of the class is occupied with other matters) and spared the practice of certain skills across a number of media. This type of software is occasionally used as an 'electronic blackboard' demonstrating a method to obtain the right answer in an attractive and often tuneful manner. The question that you, as coordinator, need to answer is whether this is the best use of an expensive and scarce resource.

As Judith Judd points out in *Children, Computers and the National Curriculum:*

'It is more important for children to become skilled in general purpose computer applications than to spend time practising spelling tests. Skilled exploitation of a spreadsheet, graphics package or desktop publishing programmes ... can improve personal productivity dramatically and is also transferable between topics.'

Some teachers may be persuaded to use the computer in ways which extend children's skills in using their imaginations by composing written texts, creating graphics, generating and solving problems, devising programs and investigating data. Ways in which this might be achieved are explored in the final part of this chapter.

Those who react negatively to the idea that children can be taught by computers are more enthusiastic about the concept of children themselves teaching computers routines and procedures. This is the concept behind **Logo**. **Logo** and **turtle graphics** are widely spoken of as important elements in IT work in primary classrooms. Many references to such work are contained in the National Curriculum (Mathematics, Technology, Science). Teachers who have worked with children in this area report enthusiastically on the benefits for children in their development of cognition, their confidence and, by the mode of working, their ability to cooperate in problem solving situations.

In her acclaimed book *Children and Computers,* Anita Straker points out that there are three related but different aspects of the use of LOGO with young children that make it worthwhile.

- it can encourage discovery learning;
- it can help children to develop mathematical concepts;
- it can provide insight into the power of programming.

From the results of my survey, children do not seem to be getting these experiences. Whether this remains true in your case will depend in part on your own priorities and the way you use the techniques in the final part of this chapter to advantage.

Assessment

Teachers will need your support when assessing a pupil's progress in IT. There will be a number of considerations before a final decision is taken about the most appropriate tasks to provide opportunities for assessment.

In the NCET pack *Assessing IT* they anticipate teachers will need to ask:

— What aspects of IT do I want to assess?

— Where does IT enhance the curriculum?

— How familiar are the children with the application or program?

— How familiar are the children with the IT concepts covered?

— Do I understand the application or program myself?

— Can I use the non-mandatory SAT to help me?

— What other curriculum areas can I assess at the same time?

— Will I have access to be the computer when I need it?

— How will I carry out the assessment?

— What evidence of pupil progress will I need to collect?

They give further advice and even provide software which can be used to assess several SoAs. Evidence can task a variety of forms including screen dumps of children's work and teacher's notes added to children's own computer printouts.

GAINING AND ORGANISING RESOURCES

An important function in any organisation is to make the maximum use of existing resources and make new resources available to meet needs as they arise. In both hardware and software fields this job is yours. So your first approach may be to organise a survey of the ways in which computers are used in your school.

Set up a schedule (twice a week is probably all you can manage) and find out the use of each machine at that instant and why it is not being used, if that is the case. Record the results and eventually tabulate the findings for presentation in an initial report to your head. Try to impersonalise the results so that you cannot be accused of telling tales about individual members of staff (you must try to remain popular).

Present a scientific survey as an indication of the current state of computer use in your school. It is not only the use of the machines, of course, which interests you but the way in which they are being used to support the curriculum. This can also be part of your survey.

By choosing particular times for your survey (thirty minutes after break, for example) you will maximise the results you obtain for computer use. What about other times? Teachers often complain that it takes half a term to get anything done with their share of the computer. However, there are plenty of times when one or two children could be finishing off the analysis of a database or putting finishing touches to a newsletter outside lesson times. Some children love staying in at playtime during could weather and using the computer can provide a useful occupation.

Some coordinators have maximised the use of scare computer time by arranging the computer timetable to take account of periods when the classes are otherwise engaged. Games afternoons, swimming periods, and hymn practice times are obvious occasions when particular classes should not be scheduled to have the computer. This is more complex than the 'week and week about' arrangements teachers have often made for themselves — perhaps the results of your survey will give you the justification to change this to make more sustained of this resource.

Careful planning can allow groups or individuals to use the machine at times when they are not involved with the rest of the class. Look at this list. Does it suggest anything to you?

- During assembly times.
- At playtime and lunch hour.
- After school and before school starts.
- During registration, story time and whilst the class are doing PE.
- Those not going swimming could use the machine at this time.

Attracting additional funds

Producing arguments for resourcing IT will need to be one of your top priorities not least because IT is a very expensive area of activity.

In producing a budget or bid for funding you will need to take account of particular local circumstances, such as the disposition of the senior management team to computer work and the current extent of the use of existing equipment. Some issues you might find useful to pursue are:

— What is the ratio of children to computer systems in your school? How many minutes per day of IT time does this allow? What is the LEA average, what is the national ratio? Can you formulate an argument for one machine per class? Is infrequent access to computers leading to superficial and fragmented use? Is sensitive equipment being damaged by wheeling it about every day? Are there inefficiencies in timetabling? Are these the most modern machines? ('Do we at Clutterbarn Primary always have to appear to be so far behind St. Johns?', is a line some coordinators might find useful). Is there a particular group of children in the school who would especially benefit from exclusive use of the computer — justifying a better than normal ratio?

— Would the purchase of *ROAMERS* or *PIP* replace the use of floor turtles and thereby release computers for other purposes? Are areas of the curriculum dealing with angles and degrees of turn being sufficiently well taught?

— Is there a question of efficiency in the use of printers? Can you look at the ways in which time is spent queuing for access to the limited number of computers with printers attached? Are some teachers reluctant to use certain programs because of this? Are children not developing specific skills? With the availability of attractive graphics creation packages can you justify at least one colour ink-jet printer? If the quality of children's work on display is crucial to the school's image then the purchase of an ink-jet printer which will give almost laser quality printing for nearly dot-matrix prices might be an attractive option to your head. The quietness of ink-jet printing might commend it to staff. Go to your local teachers' centre and bring back a copy of the output from any printer you want your school to buy. Something with the school's and headteacher's name (if possible in the school's colours) will often do the trick. You might also argue that without hard evidence how can teachers assess and record pupils' progress?

— Do the prospectuses of neighbouring schools proudly detail their computer equipment? Parents are often impressed by such details. Could the school brochure of newsletter by improved with the help of new equipment? If you can persuade your head that there is an advantage in such matters your path may become smoother.

— What provision does each subject coordinator make for the purchase of IT equipment and software? Does the Maths coordinator order *LOGO* chips, or the History coordinator the *Landmarks* programs as part of their budgets? Do you have *WRITE* through the English coordinator or *Smart* from the Art & Design requisition? If not, does this happen in other schools? If you are forced to support other areas this may well be a powerful argument for enchanced funding.

— Does your school operate a number of computers with incompatible software? Do you need to buy multiples of successful software to run on different computers? Additional funding will be needed if this is the case and you are unable to take advantage of site-licence agreements.

— If you need new software make sure that you can answer detailed questions about it. Some companies will distribute new material 'on approval' to inform decisions about purchasing. You should also read manuals and reviews of software in the TES and Child Education and talk to LEA advisors and HE tutors.

— Use National Curriculum requirements to enhance your arguments. If children need to be able to find and present.

— retrieve text and amend it using a word processing program;

— retrieve an image and amend it:

— replay a musical composition and improve it;

than they will have to have the means to do so. And this not just once but as part of their everyday experience.

quotation from working towards level 4 Non-Statutory Guidance Technology AT5

IT budget requests

Your budget request should be quite clear about what benefits can be expected from various levels of funding. It should be divided into three sections.

1. Rationale

This section should briefly describe the contribution IT currently makes to the quality of children's learning in your school, its potential for the further and the money spent on IT in previous years. The curriculum areas that are currently supported through work in IT, the ratio of children of computers, and the type of machine the school possesses may also form part of this section.

2. Repair, maintenance and consumables

An annual maintenance contract on each system may be the best option. Ask for à quote to cover printers and other accessories. An insurance policy will also be essential if you want teachers to take computers home at the weekend and holiday times.

When you have worked out a budget for repairs and insurance you need to consider requesting other sums under the heading. Maintenance means being able to continue to do the things next year, that you did in this. Thus you need to take account of depreciation and replacement costs, and put money aside each financial year to pay for the eventual replacement of your existing machines.

If the syllabus has changed you will still want to offer the same degrees of support in a variety of curriculum areas and topic work. Ask for money rather than specific titles of programs, as a details will not become apparent until after teachers have held their topic planning meetings.

Finally, remember you will need to work out the cost of consumables. Just how much computer paper, printer ribbons, or cartridges will you need? Do not forget floppy discs, batteries and any special paper for your colour ink-jet printer.

3. Development

In this part of the budget bid you demonstrate the benefits which would accrue to the children if additional money was spent on IT equipment or software. The most appropriate of the arguments presented at the start of this section are relevant alongwith any needs revealed in discussion with class teachers.

'The lower juniors consider that...'

'The equipment in the nursery is particularly prone to breakdown and Mrs. Bright feels...'

'The Yr 6 teams were telling me...'

or use 'ghosts':

'The government expects us to...'

'Parents have often commented that...'

'HMI always make a point of commenting on....'

or use National Curriculum pressures to your advantage:

'IT skills appear in the National Curriculum documents for .....subjects'

'The SAT results for our school show that more work will be needed in....'

If you intend to make a case for the purchase of one or more additional pieces of equipment, have all the details to hand. No one can then shelve your request claiming the need to wait for further information. Get local dealers to send you details of lease-purchase agreements which would avoid meeting the costs of buying capital equipment form a single year's budget.

If you are going to act as a resource for your staff you in turn will need to develop contacts and sources of help. Personal contacts and sources of information are built up slowly through attending courses and building up relationship with those in equivalent positions to yourself. However, for newcomers some general help is at hand. A local network of IT coordinators may exist already and can help in sorting out local problems with common software and finding out about good quality INSET.

MOTIVATING STAFF

Without objectives you don't know what to do, without priorities you don't know what to do first and without planning you don't know when to do it!

The most crucial part of your role is to motivate, cajole and persuade staff to work together in IT just as in any other area of the curriculum. Your best performance indicator as a coordinator will be the extent to which you achieve objectives in this area. There are a number of formal and informal ways to induce staff to cooperate. These are summarised as follows:

— **Work towards the end of making each member of the staff an expert in ONE application. Then they can share their expertise.**

— **Developing a whole-school policy — not enshrined in a static document but a commentary on continuing discussion.**

— **Whole-school INSET days** can allow staff time to discuss and have access to new machines and a variety of software. Visiting speakers bring a new perspective on the value of activities, and frequently say things that you may not be able to say. Problems may be discussed which were not previously aired, issues may arise involving different areas of the school, and unthought of cooperation may result.

— **INSET days** can be used as the opportunity for new beginnings and therefore must be properly through out to maximise their effectiveness. Any guest speaker will need to be properly briefed on the current activities of the school. Some suggestions for the best use of INSET time can be found in earlier chapters.

— **Incidental INSET** can arise from time to time when you have the opportunity to show individual teachers features of a machine or software. These opportunities occasionally arise in the solution of everyday problems, but they may also come from a deliberate tactic on your behalf to be in the right place at the right time.

Some approaches IT coordinators have used in order to gain the support of colleagues:

— Organised INSET days.

— Arranged regular times to be available for consultation.

— Supported teachers' own applications to attend LEA/HE INSET.

— Put on demonstrations at lunchtimes

— Advised at team/year group curriculum planning meetings.

— Checked and commented on teachers' termly work forecasts.

— Worked alongside teachers in their classrooms.

— Arranged visits to other schools to see IT in action.

— Arranged for the loan of computers for teachers to use at home.

— Put up displays of children's IT work in other areas of the school.

— Arranged software loans for trials.

Some coordinators have been successful by setting up a computer in the staffroom at lunchtime once a fortnight. Such occasions could consist of a software demonstration by you or simply provide an opportunity for individual staff to try out something with you close at hand to help.

Can you find someone on the staff with whom you can share some responsibilities and take over some of their duties in return? This might increase the chance of being in the right place at the right time, just when teachers feel the need for IT to help them!

Universities and colleges along with Teachers' Centres and LEAs often offer INSET opportunities in IT. It can be a most successful strategy for the IT coordinator to support the application of other teachers to go on such courses. Your support will serve a number of purposes: it demonstrates the value of the course at it comes with your stamps of approval, it spreads the level of expertise in IT matters amongst the staff, it demonstrates your willingness to take a back seat yourself and it shows your sense of responsibility in arranging training for your staff.

It also follows that as a result you may gain another voice in support of the project or software under consideration. It might also enhance your own chances of acceptance next time a course arises for something in which you are interested.

The results of my survey show that methods of training used in the past have not been as effective as many would like in persuading teachers to use IT to support children's learning across the curriculum. The steps teachers have been asked to take are perhaps just too big and they have been asked to take them far too quickly. Jane Devereux suggests that for some children

'.....the use of other, more familiar technologies might provide a safer, smaller steps for those children a little daunted by the computer itself.

She goes on to show ways in which IT other than computers can be used to support primary science. Perhaps such simple steps might be recommended to some coordinators trying to help teachers who are overfaced by technical complexities.

It has been argued that another criticism of INSET both in school, and off the premises, has been the deficit model it has used. The deficit model says to teachers

'You lack certain technical knowledge and skills.'

'Come on this course and I will show you how to connect up this system; configure this machine; run this program.'

Such training has largely been characterised by telling participants which button to press and when, and how to operate accessories. It has not called upon the professional experience of teachers, nor used their motivation to help children learn, which is their first calling. It has therefore been less effective than it might have.

An alternative model, which is possibly more successful, concentrates on building the need for IT and presents it as a solution to teachers' own problems. As well as some technical help and training, the core of your effort should be in helping teachers to understand that IT can support children's learning in various areas of the curriculum. Thus **attending topic planning meetings** to suggest the **appropriate** use of computers, looking at forecasts of teachers' work and showing ways in which computers can help them to **achieve their own ends**, is likely to be more effective and longer lasting, than any amount of technical instruction.

If you adopt this strategy further ideas will commend themselves to you. **You will arrange for staff to visit schools** in the district with a brief not to centre on the technical wizardry of the resident teachers but to see if their use of IT proffers any solutions to your teachers' problems, such as individualising work for certain children, handling information in pie charts and graphs, emphathising with children of the past, helping children understand the movements of the planets, creating perfectly lettered 3-D titles to show off children's work.

You will obtain 'on approval' software for teachers to try out in their own classrooms. Ask them to write a few words on whether it helped with their classwork. You will display infant computer work in the juniors and vice-versa to demonstrate its value in different areas of school.

The source of motivation lies in utilising teachers' desires to serve children to the best of their ability.

The influence of IT is wide than just appraising the support which can be given to various programs of study, or the best way to use a variety of software. Computers can alter the way curriculum content is organised, the sequence and frequency of certain topics, the pace of learning and the way in which learning tasks place. In many school consideration of the influence of such curriculum development is a long way off. Effective curriculum coordinators may hasten the day when these issues take centre stage.

REFERENCES

Devereux, Jade. Using IT, other than computers, to support primary science in *Primary Science Review,* 20 Dec, 1991.

Judd, Judith. *Children, Computers and the National Curriculum,* NCET, 1991.

Morrison, A *Information Technology in Primary Schools,* a research review for the Scottish Education Department, ESRC, 1988.

NCET. Assessing IT-Curriculum support materials, NCET, Coventry, 1992.

Straker, Anita, *Children using Computers,* Blackwell, 1989.

12

ART IN THE CURRICULUM

REVIEW YOUR CURRENT POSITION

As a coordinator, your first task will be to gather evidence to help you to make a judgement concerning the quality and quantity of planning and provision for art in your school. You may be fortunate and discover all that is needed is a common approach to planning and recording since content and resources are appropriate and stimulating.

However, you may not be so fortunate but, starting with a positive approach. look, for the range of expertise across the staff. Find someone doing something you like and bring it to the attention of others. There is a wealth of talent amongst teachers, your job is to uncover it and to highlight the positive. If you have a member of staff who makes an identical thumb-pot hedgehog with every child, this is a start. Think how you can persuade her to share her thumb-pots expertise with other colleagues. You could then go on to discuss children's progress in ciay work, its development and opportunities. Similarly the teacher who does some tie-dying may not be thinking of textiles and dyes as creatively or as purposefully as you do, but you can enlist that specific expertise and use it initially to share a technique with other staff and later as a route into staff development.

Remember at this stage you are reviewing the current position and trying to convince colleagues that the development of an active whole-school approach to art is desirable. In the next phase, you are going to help them to achieve it.

Defining together your values, purpose and goals

Recently there has been an enthusiasm for an 'outsider' to visit your school (or cluster of schools) and instruct you on a range of art techniques and methods of classroom organisation. Although these are important it is the purpose of teaching which should be decided upon before the details of the organisation, as Robin Alexander emphasises in *Policy and Practice in Primary Education.*

Therefore you need to ask yourself and your colleagues:

- Why are you teaching art?
- What is the function of art for children?
- How does are relate to the rest of the curriculum?

In other words:

- What is your purpose?
- What are your values?
- What are your goals?

In defining the purpose of art education in your school you have to consider with colleagues, what your shared vision is for art education in your school. I am stressing the notion of *in your school* since due account must be taken of the particular children and staff and, at a large stage, of the particular accommodation and resources.

WHY TEACH ART?

Art is now established as a subject in its own right in the National Curriculum. It has to be taught. You may feel that you would prefer to support your initiatives in art by referring to a list of aims in official documents, but you will not find any in the Programmes of Study. Therefore clarification of aims with staff will probably centre around such matters as:

- the development of the skills of art, namely drawing, use of colour, painting, primary, modelling, the use of textiles and textures;
- the development of visual literacy and appreciation;
- the appreciation of the work of other artists from a variety of cultures and styles;
- the ability to verbalise personal responses to art — to know and use effectively the language of art; line, colour, tone, shape, pattern, form and texture;

— the opportunity for personal expression and creative endeavour.

Central to art education is observation, usually visual although (as some art galleries have demonstrated) exploration of surface texture, shape and form can be successfully achieved in carefully organised displays for the blind and partially sighted. Observation is an important skill in many curricular areas but can be well taught and rehearsed in art.

Observation is more than just looking; children need to notice and given attention to the general structures and the specific details. They should be encouraged to look at shapes to discern patterns, line, similarities and differences. They should then analyse and describe their observations. Often this is done by sketching and drawing. If you compare sketching to the drafting process in English you may find that colleagues will be more willing to listen to you when you suggest that each child should keep a sketch pad or portfolio of sketches which have led to drawings, paintings, collage, modelling, printing and weaving. If not, refer them to the HMI Report on *Art and Design in Infant and Junior Schools,* published in 1990, which is also very convincing regarding quality resourcing and curriculum planning.

There is a very good case for making observation and drawing your central focus for development. Geoff Southworth made the point forcefully in his article on *Art in the Primary School:*

'Seeing is not a frill, it is not peripheral, it is CENTRAL. To ignore the visual world and the language of vision is to disregard an important area of knowledge'.

In their books on *Art in the Early Years* Rob Barnes and Margaret Morgan have ably demonstrated that art experience has a crucial role in children's educational entitlement. They each place emphasis on the development of observation and drawing. I recently asked a number of Art coordinators to consider:

— What is the purpose of teaching art?

— What do we value in art education?

— What is central to art education in our school?

There answers are presented here as a starting point for discussion in your school.

1. **Our purposes**

For each child to experience art education that will:

— develop their skills of art — drawing, painting, printing, use of colour, use of textiles, 3-D modelling;

— develop their visual perception, visual literacy and appreciation;

— develop appreciation of the work of other artists;

— provide opportunities for personal expression and creative endeavour;

— enable them to use the language of art confidently.

2. **We value:**

— quality of provision;

— quality of response;

— quality in resources;

— quality of outcomes;

— confidence to develop their own ideas;

— confidence to appraise the work of other artists;

— knowledge of media and the possibilities for development;

— a cross-curricular approach to art;

— use of the environment as a stimulus for development.

3. **Central to art education in our school**

— observation

— drawing - sketching, drafting, editing.

Your defined purposes are not only a set of aims (although the direction they will give is crucial) but also indicate the quality, the strength, the extent, the depth, the sincerity of the commitment to developing art in your school.

Traditionally, the aspects of art work included in the primary school curriculum have been drawing, painting, use of colour, printing, modelling, textiles and textures. In addition to this the Programmes of Study also refer to photography and computer graphics.

There is also great emphasis through the strands in each attainment target for teachers to use the work of a variety of other artists.

Strands in AT1 — Recording what has been seen, imagined or remembered: visual perception

— Gathering and using resources and materials

— Using different materials and techniques in practical work

— Reviewing and modifying work

Strands in AT2 — Knowledge of different kinds of art and the development of visual literacy

— Knowledge of different periods, cultures and traditions in art, and the work of influential artists

— Applying knowledge of the work of other artists to their own work.

Your vision may be that of a school filled with stimulating nooks and crannies, in which children are earnestly engaged in sketching and drafting their skill-life representations of tortured-looking lumps of wood. But that may not be reality at present. So how are you going to effect the change?

Art 5—16: Blue Book

The Gulbenkian Report (1982) argued that the arts make essential contributions in six main areas of educational responsibility namely:

1. in developing the full variety of children's intelligence;
2. in developing the capacity for creative thought and action;
3. in the education of feeling and sensibility;
4. in the exploration of values;
5. in understanding cultural changes and differences;
6. in developing physical and perceptual skills.

VISUAL LITERACY AND THE LANGUAGE OF ART

One of the difficulties that you may encounter is colleagues who find it difficult to articulate their view of the role of art in school. This could be due to inexperience or their simply may have never thought about it before and may need encouragement. It could well be, however, a lack of knowledge of the appropriate language or ovscerity in its usage. So you may need to develop some activities which generate responses to questions such as:

— What is art?

— How do we recognise and describe it?

— Can we compare different experiences, forms of art such as painting, drawing, textiles, sculpture?

Any consideration of art education for children, its values and purposes, will emphasise the development of visual literacy (recognising, being able to describe and respond to the elements of art — see below), the specific skills of observing and drawing, empowering a child to express their ideas, images and emotions, and hence the development of the individual.

Five steps towards promoting your vision of art in your school.

1. Informally 'visit' each member of staff to discover and discuss some positive art work in each classroom. Alternatively, select something positive in three or four classroom (anonymous or identified) to bring to the attention of other staff.

2. Choose children's work to demonstrate at least one activity for each of the main aspects of art — work, namely drawing, painting, use of colour, printing, modelling, texture or textiles.

   Pick our points that:

   — illustrate purpose in the artistic activity

   — require planning — including progression

   — involve specific organisational details.

3. Elaborate through further discussion, the media used and your colleagues' aspirations.

4. Make it obvious why you like certain features. Always supplement what may be unfamiliar terms for non-specialists with examples, So 'mixed-media' would be followed by 'like in this work where the child has used both calk and ink'.

5. Circulate a summary of discussions using headings such as drawing, printing etc., and a note of activities undertaken by staff. These will be useful examples which may stimulate both replication and development.

You'll need to ensure that the language of art is developed rapidly to prevent the more insecure members of staff withdrawing completely from discussions with more articulate colleagues: Many people will bow to the judgement of anyone who discusses a work of art with confidence. Some colleagues will benefit from access to the language of art so that they can express their ideas and responses with confidence themselves.

Hence, staff development is crucial if your colleagues are to be able to interpret with you the National Curriculum Attainment Targets and Programmes of Study. Sue Tallach in *First Impressions* suggests that we have a low level of visual literacy in this country, and therefore that it is AT2 (Knowledge and Understanding) which will pose the greatest challenge to primary teachers.

By visual literacy we mean recognising, describing and responding to our world and the forms of art using the language of art; Line, tone, pattern, texture, colour, shape, form and space.

The development of the range of forms of art may well be generated through one of the earlier practical activities when are work around the school was identified. Ensure that during any training activity you arrange that the full range of forms (drawing, painting, printing etc.) are referred to. With relevant language colleagues should be better able to articulate their responses to art and its purpose.

— Discuss with staff what they mean by art and under what circumstances children are regarded as 'doing art'.

— Discuss various forms of art (paintings, drawings, print including fabric, models, artefacts, photographs). Which do teachers like and why?

— Organise an art-trail around the school and the grounds. They could look for examples of art around school, including a variety of artefacts, and opportunities for art in the environment (indoors and out).

— Use published prints of the work of artists to consider a particular theme, say water, and encourage your colleagues to discuss and evaluate them.

POLICY AND PLANNING IN ART

In designing the school's policy for art you should clearly demonstrate the chain of interpretation from lofty aims and stated values to actual learning experienced by the children.

The policy should be a description of the current work going on in school and you plans forward for development. Therefore it can only be drafted after discussions with all your colleagues. In this way it will reflect your school's current provision for teaching art, the values and purposes of art education agreed with the staff, along with the general intentions of the National Curriculum and the specific requirement and content of the Art Document.

Furthermore, it must be remembered that the National Curriculum is for all children, so your document will have to ensure that provision is made for children who have special needs.

Additional points to bear in mind when planning your policy:

— the cultural diversity of artistic experience present in the school and that all children need to experience art from a variety of cultures, both Western and Non-Western (AT 2 and the PoS):

— children should not be allowed to assume that only deceased European men have produced significant work of art;

— there are female as well as male artists and works of art can be used be challenge gender stereotypes. (An example of this approach was an exhibition at the Whitworth Art Gallery, Manchester when pairs of works of art of the same from and subject matter were positioned side by side. One way by a female artist and one by a male artist. Viewers were invited to decide which was which and to consider why they made that response).

In developing your policy you have a variety of factors to address:

1. The purpose of writing the document and the values you wish to express.

2. The framework of the curriculum and was of engaging with art i.e. education in and through art; the interpretation of PoS, attainment targets, strands and end of Key Stage statements.

3. Organisation and resources (including use of locality and visits by artists).

4. Planning and recording of experience and attainment.

As you develop your policy you need to achieve that different balance between the requirements and possibilities of a National Curriculum on the one hand and the need and capabilities of your children, your colleagues and yourself. The checklists for policy development in the NCC's *Arts* 5-16 will be useful.

HOW SHOULD ART BE TAUGHT?

The whole area of art education hinges on two main approaches;

1. education in art

2. education **through** art

You will come across lots of references to the 'in' and 'through' debates.

Education **in** art has to do with the development of the technical and aesthetic qualities of art (Investigating and Making). Education through are allows for consideration of themes or subject matter and for personal and social education (Knowledge and Understanding).

The National Curriculum identifies the major aspects of art work with children as:

— **Making and Investigating:** drawing, painting, printing, use of colour, textiles, textures, 3-D modelling.

— **Knowledge and Understanding:** appreciating their won work and that of others in and from a range of contexts - time, culture, subject, mood, style, genre.

Education **in** art will involve the development of the skills of creating art such as mark-making, colour mixing, applying paint, drawing, creating a block for printing and evaluating or appraising it within its context.

Education **through art might** involve;

— using paintings, portraits and scenes to further children's understanding of historical or social conditions;

— looking at prints of paintings to do with families and homes;

— studying the prints of William Morris in order to consider the impact of technology on design.

You need to discuss at length with colleagues the advantages and disadvantages of both the 'through' and 'in' ways of engaging with art and what degree of supportive teaching is appropriate.

Education through art has largely been the favoured approach in primary school. A sensible policy will embrace both methods and this will underpin the attainment targets. Good quality art results from informed teaching. Just as we should give children access to **knowledge teaching. Just as we should give children access to** knowledge, so we should no longer be hesitant to teach the skills and techniques of observation, drawing and printing.

You cannot possibly be an expert on every aspect of art and how to teach it but you can generate ways of finding answers. Two very useful sources are:

1. for content - *World of Art* series published by Dolphin Books is a good start. It includes a book on female artists.

2. for policy - *The Arts 5-16* published by Oliver & Boyd

Planning, recording, assessment

In planning the curriculum you are reminded in the art document that the National Curriculum is intended to be broad, balanced, differentiated, relevant and it should allow for both continuity and progression. The National Curriculum (NC Art) identifies art's unique characteristics as:

— The emphasis on visual literacy.

— The practice of specific technical skills.

— The harnessing of observation, memory and feeling in order to express and communicate ideas in visual form.

— Art as a distinct body of knowledge.

— The fostering of responses to the work of artists.

The emphasis is very clear in NC Art. We need to use the Programmes of Study and the strands for planning and recording purposes and to be sure that all who teach art are familiar with these documents.

The danger of looking at the NC Art and thinking of planning and recording is that you may very quickly get locked into the grid mentality. Your overriding concern becomes that of how to design a record of planning that will fit on to A4 paper for easy photocopying and storage! However, in the quest for a way of referencing ATs, strands, and PoS do not lose sight of why you are teaching art. You will find examples of planning record sheets in the Non-Statutory Guidance (Section D).

As you are planning a whole-school approach to art provision you need to ensure that there is a clear route from your stated purposes to the practical activity. The NC Art itself acknowledges that there are different routes into planning:

— starting planning from end of Key Stage statements;

— starting from individual items in the PoS;

— starting from existing plans and 'mapping' them against the requirements;

— planning from related groupings of PoS items.

Art has often been seen only as an activity related to a topic which has generated display material. You will want to keep on displaying art work, but your intention will be lead colleagues into a planned art curriculum. This brings you back to the 'in' and 'through' debate. Teachers may well be planning art experience to complement learning in other areas through athematic approach, so that you are bound to look at the Impressionists (for example Mary Cassatt) if you have a topic on light or trees or water, or perhaps some Rasb prints if you are planning a topic on buildings. The children working on a topic on buildings are sure to make sketches, make models, explore textures by rubbings and casts, or they might print and weave. All this is art experience. It will need planning and recording.

The other approach is education 'in' art where your planning is specifically related to progress in artists' skills such as drawing from the environment, clay modelling, mono-prints. These skills have to be identified and taught.

Careful use of the NC Art document's strands, Programmes of Study and end of Key Stage statements should ensure that your planning will incorporate assessment. The crucial point for both teachers and children in appraising children's art work is that relevant language is developed and meanings shared. Currently for many children the assessment of the work whether or not it is displayed. It must go further than this to be of use to children, their parents and next year's teacher.

Some of the practical activities suggested so far should give colleagues opportunities and suggest ways of talking about art as this is central of useful assessment. Children and their teachers need to be able to discuss, describe and analyse art work. They can then appraise an individual piece of work and identify progression.

Assessment of art requires an appreciation of context. The notion of appraisal of art work within its context (which may be cultural, historic, stylistic, thematic) or form (painting, sculpture, drawing) is vital if colleagues and children are to develop their skills of appraisal and understanding.

RESOURCES

Planning and assessment need to be fully integrated with a consideration of the range, quality and organisation of resources. The quality of materials you use is very important and you should try to ensure adequate funds. Resist the temptation to order economy 'packs'. You may well find that you are buying large quantities of colours of paper, paint etc. that you do not want and do not or should not use.

At the end of this chapter is a suggested basic stock of materials for a typical primary classroom. However before making your choice here are some pointers to keep in mind:

1. If you establish in your planning that you want children to explore the use of colour you commit yourself

automatically to colour mixing. Having established this, you would then only order the primary colours (red, blue, yellow) and black and white. In *Art-4-11* Margaret Morgan gives reasons for this: namely that you would need to order two reds (scarlet or vermilion and crimson), two yellows (warms ochre and lemon) and two blues (bright cobalt and Prussian). You will need twice as much yellow and white as red and blue, and even less black. Your justification to staff for this selection might be that they cannot attempt to assess a child's use of colour if they have neither organised it nor taught the children how to mix and apply colour in paint. Additionally, when ordering pencils you need pencils in a range of strength and colours (ivory, ebony, terracotta, sepia...) but you do not need thirty of each for every class!

2. 'Rainbow' packs of paper may be wasteful because they can result in everyone using the blue, purple and green first and having little use for the yellow and orange. Neither you nor the children are increasing your levels of visual literacy by only using these more startling 'nursery' colours.

3. It is better for you and your colleagues to select the colours for the children to work on or for display purposes. Greys, beiges, off-whites, blacks, interesting ranges of grey-blues, muted greens and earthy browns encourage discrimination and subtlety of choice. These colours will also suit the use of the environment (natural and man made materials). There used to be a wonderful pinky beige sugar paper which was marvellous for chalk pastels and charcoal drawings — may be you will find some ancient discarded stock.

4. Good quality drawing tools are essential. You can order some excellent boxed sets of pencils, crayons and pastels — one box per class. Again this is tied up with classroom organisation and management. You need to help staff decide:

   — How best to organise children's learning in art? — whole-class, group or individual work.

- The way to set up and use an art area with relevant materials.
- How to manage the access to and maintenance of materials.

At the stage of planning the curriculum, it is important to consider the detail of materials, organisation, storage and access. Planning goes hand in hand with discussion of how resources are organised. Usually good teachers are also good organisers. Some members of staff may have difficulties with organisation and may well feel insecure with any radical overhaul of their teaching style and methods of organisation. Therefore you will need to proceed with caution and help by your example, encouragement and support. You will want to demonstrate that if your colleagues value the notion of allowing children greater independence to select materials in an informal way and to handle them appropriately, then an adequate selection of materials will have to be available. They will need to have clean brushes, good quality scissors, clean working rollers and glue that is ready for use. You may be able to provide 'before and after' photographs of your own art area to demonstrate the organisation of equipment and materials.

- Arrange for part of an INSET day to be spent visiting a school that shares a large measure of your vision.
- Reorganise your own teaching area into the sort of environment you have in mind.
- Take some 'before and after' pictures which are always popular when used in staff meetings of INSET time.
- Collect examples of quality work produced by your children and explain how the learning situation was organised to achieve the results. Arrange for another colleague to do the same.
- Plan to involve local artists — they can work with colleagues and/or children.
- Visit a local gallery by yourself and plan how to use the gallery with children.

Specific resources

Some authorities and individual schools make successful use of visiting artists. These artists may be local craft workers or students undertaking specialist art courses. Such people are knowledgeable and enthusiastic about involving young children. If you are not fortunate enough to have this facility at present, perhaps you can liaise with other schools to buy-in to such a similar scheme in the future.

Liaising with your local secondary school is well worth the effort. You will need to be involved in planning the transition from Key Stage 2 to Key Stage 3. At the same time you may be able to use of the expertise of the art teacher and some of their specialist resources.

Below is a basic collection of art materials for a class of thirty-five primary school children. It is not an exhaustive list but it does provide variety. Remember they key word is **quality** not **quantity**.

Range of pencils - boxed sets to include range of soft and hard leads and coloured drawing pencils e.g. Derwent Drawing Pencils (6) or Faber-Castell Portrait colours.

— craypas

— oil pastels

— fixative spray

— brushes

— printing ink

— chalk pastels

— charcoal

— watercolours

— diffusers (or air-sprayers)

— cut paper sizes A4/A3/A2

Quality - cartridge, sugar, tracing } Colours — carefully selected

— sketch pads – bought or made

— brushes – 0-11 range of sizes, short-handled

— long-handled brushes

— large 'decorators' brushes

— trays for printing
— rollers
— polyprint tiles
— scissors - 6 right-handed, 2 left-handed and of good quality
— power paint/liquid paint - primary (red, blue, yellow) plus black and white
— glue stick and pots (e.g. collect plastic tablet pots or photo film pots)
— glue - PVA and powder

IN CONCLUSION

Everyone enjoys artistic experiences, including your colleagues. Remember that throughout history and across cultures people have enjoyed art. They have experimented with ways of representing their world, their lives, their feelings in drawings, paint, sculpture and textiles.

Achievements in artistic endeavours are used as benchmarks of civilisations. Your colleagues will be encouraged by your commitment and enthusiasm. You will be able to facilitate their work with support and leadership in planning and resourcing.

The art experience of the children in your school will be one of the hallmarks of the quality of education provided there. Visual literacy will enrich their lives.

REFERENCES

Alexander, R *Policy and Practice in Primary Education,* Routledge, London, 1992.

Barnes, R. *Teaching Art to Young Children,* 4-9, Unwin Hyman, London, 1987.

Morgan, M. *Art 4-11,* Suffolk Country Council, 1988.

NCC. *The Arts 5-16,* Oliver & Boyd, London, 1990.

Southworth, G, Art in the Primary School: Towards First Principles in *Journal of Art and Design Education,* Vol. 1, No. 2, 1982.

Tallach, S. in Neumark, V *First Impressions,* TES Curriculum Update, May 1992.

BIBLIOGRAPHY

Casson, M. *The Craft of the Potter,* BBC, London, 1991.

Clement, R. *The Art Teachers Handbook,* Stanley Thornes, Cheltenham, 1989.

Fitzsimmons, S. *Start with Art,* Blackwell, Oxford, 1991.

Gentle, K. *Teaching Painting in the Primary School,* Cassell, London, 1993.

Hargreaves, D. *Children and the Arts,* OUP, 1989.

Hollebone, S. *Screen Printing,* A & C Black, London, 1980.

Jordan Hill College. *Art in the Primary School* — a series of useful booklets.

Kellogg, R. *Analysing Children's Art,* National Press, San Francisco USA, 1970.

Lancaster, J. *Art in the Primary School,* Routledge, London, 1990.

Lancaster J. *Art, Craft & Design in the Primary School,* NSEAD, 1990.

Lowenfeld, V. & Brittain, W. *Creative and Mental Growth,* Macmillan, New York, 1982.

Read, H. *Education Through Art,* Faber, London, 1958.

Other useful organisations

Professional Association:

National Society for Education in Art & Design, NSEAD, 7a High Street, Corsham Wiltshire, SN13 0ES.

National Foundation for Arts Education, NFAE, The Spendlove Centre, Enstone Road, Charlbury, Oxford, OX7 3PQ. Tel: 060 8 811488.

13

THE MUSIC CURRICULUM

STEPS TO PRIMARY MUSIC

With the introduction of music to the National Curriculum there exist a statutory framework for music in all primary schools. This requires the implementation of Programmes of Study for each Key Stage. Pupils need to demonstrate skills, knowledge and understanding within the attainment targets of Performing and Composing and Listening and Appraising.

Because many primary schools are limited in what they can offer to children's music education, there is clearly a need to find ways of helping teachers to plan, implement and monitor Programmes of Study. Many teachers lack formal training in music and feel that they are not equipped to develop music in the curriculum. Whilst most LEAs have music support services, the specific needs no individual primary schools will be best met by having a member of staff with the appropriate skills and expertise to help individual teachers and to coordinate work in the music curriculum across the whole-school.

What is special about the music coordinator ?

The music coordinator in the primary school might be:

— a specialist musician on the school staff;

— a non-specialist with some music skills, knowledge, understanding and a willingness to learn;

— a teacher shared between a group of schools;

— a part-time visiting musician, employed through a support service such as a LEA music centre.

Whichever of these best describes your position, music should be taught and organised in relation to the curriculum as a whole, and by teachers who know the children as individuals. Your main task will be to act 'bringer-together' of a variety of approach, activities and materials. Your aims will include linking music with other curricular areas, establishing music programmes in realistic and structured ways, assisting and encouraging colleagues and other curriculum coordinators.

MAKING A START

Coordinating, managing and taking the leading position in shaping a music curriculum for the primary school carries many challenges. Bringing staff together to talk about and produce a compilation of music objectives will not in itself result in a neat path leading to their achievement, but it is the first step in the construction of a whole-school music policy.

This chapter will help you consider some basic questions, such as:

— Do you see yourself as a specialists a facilitator, prompter, monitor, motivator...? They are all valid roles.

— How does your headteacher define your responsibilities?

— What do other members of staff expect from you?

— Is the School currently meeting the children's needs in music? What evidence do you have for this?

— How best can you oversee and estimate the breadth and effectiveness of music teaching in your school? How much non-contact time has been budgeted for this?

— How can you create lists of priorities such as content, resources, recording, assessment?

— If a scheme for music already exists in your school, are all the staff familiar with it? How are the new staff introduced to it? If it does not exist, how can you create such a scheme?

— How can you determine that, in music, colleagues and yourself work in the best possible partnership?

— What guidance and support can you give and how can you give it?

— What in-service activities in music can you arrange for the staff?

Some practical starting points

Take a careful look at music in your school and draw up a series of aims and objectives for teaching music in the future.

Making music in school should produce happiness and satisfaction for all who take part and all who listen. It may, on the other hand, take years to comprehend the basic elements of music, both structural and expressive. These can be achieved by taking part in and by responding to a broad ranged of music activities developed in a progressive pattern or taking place at the same time.

Take care that your programmes of work are not too stifling: flexibility is crucial. Your children will progress in music at different rates, at different ages, as in other subject areas. Many teachers will feel unsure and lacking in music skills and knowledge. However, with guidance from you and some training, they should be able to give children first-hand experience of varied types of music and music-making, providing stimulation and challenges for all pupils.

A number of factors may influence your approach. Among these are:

— vertical or single age grouping of children;

— the building (open plan classrooms are not ideal for noisy music-making!);

— pupils whose mother-tongue is not English (the singing of songs can assist the learning of language);

— the school's practice on formal or thematic lesson approaches.

Whilst drawing up a set of written aims in music, it might be worthwhile looking into the possibility of producing a short Music Handbook. This would list the school's philosophy in music education, its aims and basic strategies. The Handbook would be used by staff, governors, parents and visitors.

NATIONAL CURRICULUM MUSIC

Implementing the National Curriculum probably stands out sharply from our many other music concerns. Teachers will need to relate the National Curriculum ATs and PoS in music to their own teaching situations. The ATs can be seen as music objectives against which we should plan. The statutory PoS are broad enough to allow us to produce our own schemes of work. One result of the National Curriculum in music could be that many teachers feel relieved that at last the crucial decisions and burden of what has to be taught are laid down nationally. This gives us the opportunity to concentrate on drawing up our own schemes of work — according to our music resources, human and physical — in order to meet those objectives.

Action now

An immediate task is to catalogue all the music resources available to your teachers and note their type, number, condition and location. Start a programme to repair those in poor condition and identify gaps in provision (see section on Resources).

Sketch out early plans for record-keeping, evaluation and assessment in music (see section on Assessment).

Check that liaison takes place between members of staff working on integrated programmes including music. See where you can help staff and pupils in the organisation of music at assembly, end term events and concerts.

You will need to organise timetables for pupils who have instrumental lessons and cooperate and maintain close contact with their visiting tutors.

THE MUSIC COORDINATOR AS ORGANISER

You will be responsible for organising all aspects of music in your school and will need to be aware of current trends and philosophy in music education.

Schemes of work

Your aim is to formulate and agree a comprehensive and thoroughly prepared scheme of work, fitting in with the school's overall aims and objectives and National Curriculum requirements. This scheme should be based upon the philosophy embodied in the National Curriculum Report for Music which states:

'The study of music as a foundation subject should provide for the progressive development of :

— awareness and appreciation of organised sound patterns;
— skills in movement, such as motor coordination and dexterity, vocal skills and skills in aural imagery (imagining and internalising sounds), acquired through exploring and organising sound;
— sensitive, analytical and critical responses to music;
— the capacity to express ideas, thoughts and feelings through music;
— awareness and understanding of traditions, idioms and musical styles from a variety of cultures, times and places; and
— the experience of fulfilment which derives from striving for the highest possible artistic and technical standards.'

Teachers will need to find space within the primary school curriculum to that these aims may be met in the following ways:

— pupils should practise and learn a repertoire of songs from a variety of cultures;
— pupils should become skilled in using both pitched and unpicked percussion instruments;
— pupils should become musically literate and able to create and notate music;
— pupils should listen to and be able to discuss a wide variety of different kinds of music.

The basic musical concepts so such a scheme must include:

— **rhythm** : the movement side of music in time;
— **pitch** : the height and depth of sounds;
— **melody** : musical sounds in succession;
— **harmony** : sounds combined together into chords;
— **form** : the shape or structure of music;
— **expression** : all those things, such as speed, tone, touch, phrasing, blowing, etc. which make a performance interesting and personal.

A SAMPLE SCHEME FOR PRIMARY SCHOOLS

Starting points

The policy document you produce should state boldly that the principal aim of music teaching is to encourage and develop understanding, sensitivity and enjoyment of music in children through playing an active part in performing, composing and listening. A wide variety of different musical experiences can be fostered through clear teaching techniques that develop in our pupils an awareness of sound and the ability to identify, collect, imitate, classify and describe sounds.

The scheme should include suggestions of a good repertoire of songs. The singing of ostinati, descants, rounds and simple part songs can be closely landed with rhythm patterns, ostinati and drones played on pitched and unpitched percussion instruments. The development of musical literacy will include rhythm and pitch notation, signs and symbols taught as a relevant and integral part of practical; music-making. You should encourage teachers to store pieces of music created by the children, by means of symbolic, graphic of staff notation, or by memory, cassette recorder or computer.

Listening to music of different styles and cultures is best presented as an active process, with frequent assessment procedures, and seen from the pupils' point of view as part of a progressive structure of learning. There are many cross-curricular links between music and other subjects: these should be identified in your document so that the curriculum can be presented as a whole.

The following is intended to be a starting point in constructing an appropriate scheme of work.

Key Stage 1

— Listen to everyday sounds inside the classroom, in the school environment, in the local neighbourhood and on audio tape, and make sounds by using voice, body and other objects by clapping clicking, humming, striking. Discriminate between loud/soft; high/low; short/long; sharp/smooth.

— Collect a number of sounds on a tape recorder and find a way of writing them down by using picture symbols.

— Experiment with a variety of sounds using pitched and unpitched percussion instruments.

— Build up a repertoire of songs and singing games. Allow the children to hear the song singing and encourage the development of good tone.

— Use pitched and unpitched percussion to pick out the rhythm of part of a song — develop ostinati. Use flash cards to allow children to practise skills in recognising rhythm and pitch notation.

— Create and notate pieces of music — possibley as a response to a poem or a story. Allow the children to experiment with different sounds and instruments. Demonstrate use of the pentatonic scale.

— Develop rhythmic awareness by action songs, body movement, folk dance.

— Listen to music from a wide variety of cultures and countries. Listening might be linked to other activities in the curriculum but should be of fairly short duration. Let the children listen *for* something. Perhaps take a theme or a composer each week.

Key Stage 2

Singing

Develop breath control, in tune singing , vowel shapes and clear voice production. Be aware of the range of a song and aim to develop a good sense of pitch. Sing unaccompanied whenever possible. Develop part singing by good unison — round — descant — part-singing.

Rhythm

More advanced music/action songs and games. Improvise rhythmic sounds and rhythmic accompaniments using both voice and instruments.

Notation

Allow the children to find their own way of writing down rhythm and melody. Graphic scores might be used to record a piece of creative music making. Introduce staff notation gradually — probably by using a three line stave linked with tonic sol-fa.

Composition

Use of pentatonic scale. Group work developing themes and responding to pictures, poems, stories etc. This will need to be carefully directed whilst allowing the children to develop their own ideas. Allow time for the children to *perform* their composition. Link this work to listening to music from other cultures, past centuries or the contemporary scene.

Pitch

Further exploration, using object in the environment, voice sounds and musical instruments of high/low, repeat notes, steps and leaps between notes. Investigate melodic shapes with hand movements and drawings. Echoes: by singing or playing on an instrument.

Listening

Identifying voices and instruments. Responding to, and discussing, the moods and style of a variety of music. Developing an awareness of the principal concepts of music.

RESOURCES

Individual schools will vary considerably in the facilities and resources which are available. You need to be conscious of what is desirable in order to implement the agreed music scheme.

The sample scheme above requires a good selection of pitched and unpitched percussion instruments. For your scheme some instruments will be essential, whilst others may be added as the work progresses.

Coordinators should follow the principles outlined in Chapter One to set up a bid for a budget in music education. You might aim to equip your school according to a schedule such as:

Basic classroom instruments (untuned)

Woodblocks — including two-tone woodblocks, wooden agogo, claves, temple or tulip block

Tambourines

Tambours

Maracas

Castanets (handled)

Triangles (small and large)

Bells - including Indian bells, stick jungles or sleigh bells

Cymbal (suspended)

Guiro or rasp

Basic classroom percussion instruments (tuned)

Set of chime bars (flat based)

Xylophone (alto to begin with)

Glockenspiel (alto to begin with)

Bass resonator bars

A variety of beaters — including felt-headed, plastic, wood and rubber

Other useful instruments

The include instruments from Eastern and Western cultures and will bring variety and colour to music-making in your school.

agogo bells	chocola	khartal
vibra slap	flexatone	whistles
wind chimes	dhalak	kalimabas (thumb pianos)
rainmaker	shekere	cane rattles
gungroos	cabasa	kokoriko/click clack
frame drums	kaluba drums	talking drums
tabla drums	snare drums	bongo drums
	gato drums	

tenor/ alto metallophone (diatonic)

bass xylophone / metallophone (diatonic)

soprano xylophone / glockenspiel

Further considerations about equipment and resources

Appropriate space is necessary for music activities to take place. It may vary from a small area which may be used for group work to much larger spaces such as the hall, where music and movement can take place.

Good quality recording equipment and playback systems are essential.

An overhead projector with screen is an advantage.

Baskets and trays are useful for storing percussion instruments.

Adjustable music stands and small desk stands will be essential for instrumental work.

Electronic keyboards and music computer programmes will add considerably to the range of opportunities you can offer.

A good quality piano, tuned and regulated is a must.

Acoustic and electric guitars may be useful.

Care and proper storage of instruments and equipment are vital. Many infant departments develop music corners or areas where pupils can experiment with instruments and make a variety of sounds. It is desirable that pupils have access to instruments and that their care is part of the process of the musical education of the children. One or more trolleys for storing instruments are invaluable and allow instruments to be transported easily to different areas of the school.

You should become familiar with television and radio programmes and bring relevant information on these to the attention of the teachers.

Training

You will need to organise a programme of training for colleagues. Such training sessions may be school based or held or held out of school time. In both instances headteachers and colleagues should be informed in advance of dates and times, particularly if use of non-contact time has timetable implications.

A whole-staff workshop can be a fruitful and enjoyable starting point. Such sessions ought to be carefully devised, taking into consideration the musical skills and the fears of colleagues. Workshop can introduce teachers to a range of resources and instruments, establish confidence, and include practical hands-on experience. Practical advice on the organisation on such sessions is offered is Chapter Two.

Assessment

Most primary teachers have little experience of objectively assessing children's performance in music. This contrasts sharply with the well-known system of graded examinations in practical and theoretical music dating back to the nineteenth century and amongst the oldest forms of assessment by public examination. There are no music SATs; but a simple, unfussy and efficient scheme of music assessment should prove helpful to teachers, pupils and parents. The assessment policy you adopt must have clearly stated criteria relating to the National Curriculum. The main principles should be:

— the methods of assessment must be valid, reliable and conducted with sensitivity;

— assessment procedures should be designed to match the needs of your pupils;

— assessment of musical skills should be continuous, taking note of the development of competence as well as the acquisition of new skills;

— the process as well as the product should be assessed;

— children's musical attainments should take into account their activities as individuals and as members of a group;

— any extra curricular activity or instrumental tuition should be taken into consideration;

— as well as assessing technical skills, we must never omit the pupil's qualities of musicianship, creativity and imagination.

Music assessment is to be founded on the fourteen statements for the end of Key Stages 1 and 2. These differ from the SoA with their ten-level set of criteria. As there are no levels there can be no AT 'score' in music. In place of scores, teachers make judgements based on the accumulation of evidence, including that from the child's previous teachers. Answers to the following questions will be essential in order for teachers to make these judgements:

— What evidence will be needed , e.g. from a song, a composition, a discussion?

— Are further criteria necessary?

- Have end of Key Stage teachers discussed these judgements with other members of staff?
- Have they taken into account the 2:1 weighting in favour of AT1?
- Is the evidence both manageable and useful? If not, what changes can you bring about?
- Have the teachers shared vocabulary and criteria in their discussion of pupil achievement? Have they moderated each other's judgements?
- How much have the pupils been involved in assessing their own performances?
- Have the parents received information, not only about their child's progress against national standards, but also about the music curriculum?
- Have you ensured that the same approach to teacher assessment and reporting to parents has been used for music, art and physical education?

Music assessment can take place during class music-making activities such as composing, singing and playing. We need to be concerned with the cultivation of music skills, concepts, understanding and attitudes. Music assessment helps to show us the individual's strengths and weaknesses in, for example, singing in a group or coordinating the use of arm-hand-beater on percussion instruments. It enables us to be more perceptive about our future music planning.

Records of assessment are best simple ad short, enabling you to chart the child's progress in curriculum music and to underpin the annual report sent to parents. It will be advantageous for you to look for any further support materials assisting music assessment from the Schools Examinations and Assessment Council.

Non-classroom activities

Your role will be crucial in the organisation of extra-curricular music. This will often depend on the collective expertise of the staff although extra help may be available through peripatetic instrumental/vocal services. You will have to develop an overview of the work done both by staff in school and visiting musicians. You will be responsible for drawing together such work in the organisation of choirs, and various instrumental ensembles.

Music for the school assembly may provide opportunities for performing by groups or individuals or listening to music on tape or records. A mixture of both is desirable and may be used and selected to reflect work in other areas of the curriculum.

School productions and concerts need careful planning and you will inevitably play a key role. The time you devote to such activities can pay dividends for you personally. Your ability to manage other adults successfully, coordinate tasks performed by parents and other teachers and motivate children to give of their best will be valued — not least because the school's public reputation rests in your hands two or three times a year.

THE MUSIC COORDINATOR AS COMMUNICATOR

Successful and effective music coordinators must develop the ability to communicate with a wide range of people. Crucial to all aspects of the work will be support from various people.

Work with the headteacher

The quality of the provision for music in the primary school curriculum will depend upon the basis of the agreement you can reach with your headteacher. There are resource implications to every aspect of policy:

— Make sure that the policy for music is reflected in the aims of the school and presented as a priority in the school's development plan.

— Ensure, by agreement with the headteacher and school management team, that there is suitable space for music teaching.

— Musical instruments are expensive: you need to put forward a strong case and point to the benefits of budgeting over a number of years.

— You will need to negotiate non-contact time to undertake all the tasks in building a place for music eduction, and also to support your colleagues in and out of the classroom.

Working with classteachers

In order to support fellow colleagues, your main consideration will need to be one of *confidence building.* Within the staff of a primary school there may be people with some musical skills. Discover whether any teachers play an instrument, sing in a group or choir, read music, attend concerts or take part in music at church. Informal discussions with colleagues can often elicit this information more readily than a questionnaire or meeting.

It will be to your advantage to encourage the development of these musical skills in the staff. It is best done in a way which is non-threatening. Workshops with the whole staff or groups of people to impart knowledge skills and information may prove a useful starting point for this task. You should be prepared to discuss whole-school projects for musical ideas. Such discussions need to be ongoing. Regular, well-planned meetings where ideas can be shared, are necessary for the development of the work in both the short and long term. Consider these points of organisation:

— How frequently should music discussion take place?

— What agenda will there be for each meeting? Who will be invited?

— Who will decide on the agenda?

— How much time will be necessary? Lunch-time? After school? Other non-contact time?

Outside agencies

You need to make yourself aware of agencies which can act as a support to your staff. The LEA Music Advisor/Inspector will know of any peripatetic support or in-service work taking place within your locality. Look out for examples of good practice in other schools as well as regional and national courses. In your initial discussion with the senior management team make sure that provision is made for you to attend such courses.

Primary-secondary liaison can provide useful links with the music department in the local secondary school. Most comprehensive schools have a Head of Music and facilities may be available for the secondary music teacher to assist feeder primary schools, if this is appropriate.

Professional associations concerned with music education in schools can be a fruitful source of information and assistance. Particularly useful are the Incorporated Society of Musicians and the Musicians' Union (both of which have a specialist section concerned with music in education), the Music Advisers' National Association, the Schools Music Association and UK Council for Music Education and Training. (Addresses of these bodies can be found at the end of this chapter.)

IDEAS FOR A SAFE MUSIC DAY

The following suggestions are for an INSET day when all the staff meet, led by the music coordinator, in an exploration and discussion of music activities.

Aim: To provide members of staff with some basic music skills, knowledge, understanding and confidence, enabling them to try a series of short music sessions with their class.

— 'Break the ice' by sharing memories of one's own childhood experiences in music at primary school or by singing a song or two that everybody knows.

— Give plenty of encouragement.

— Build towards a 'performance' of the music activities in which you all engaged, thereby ensuring the delight, even on a small scale, of making music.

— Adopt an approach in which the staff feel (however limited their musical ability may be) they can all make a contribution to school music, by singing or playing or discussing. This can be thought of as a 'whole-staff' approach:

— Always try to cultivate a sense of musicianship at all levels of work: try to make your music activities interesting, varied and expressive.

Group activities

Set up activities for groups of teachers, say six to group. Ask them to try these out and then tell other members about them. Here are six suitable ideas to use as a starting point. You will then be able to invent, investigate and practise many more with your colleagues.

1. Create some music using voices, body sounds and any available instruments, both home-made and professional. Perhaps work to a stimulus:

   a short story

   a picture

   a short poem

   a series of moods or situations.

2. Try to invent **symbols** (dots, dashes, zig-zags. squiggles. etc.) to represent and record your music.
3. Copy voice and body sounds.
4. Try some echo games: clapping, tapping and using untuned percussion instruments.
5. Try some imitating games and question answer games just using tuned percussion instruments such as glockenspiels or xylophones.
6. Clap or tap your name to your group. Ask them all to join in. Try to record the sounds of your name using dots/blobs on paper.

Note

— Encourage everyone to have a try.

— Encourage group discussion about these musical inventions.

— What age of children do staff consider each to be suitable for?

— What ATs and level does each activity meet?

— Can we use these music activities to assess children's performance and compositional skills?

Suggestions for class activities

These are some suggestions you could use as class activities. Ask all the staff to try these and report back. They might then invent some more.

— Investigate music as part of sound generally: sounds in the classroom, school, environment; sounds heard on school visits to farms, museums, seaside, and so on.

- Investigate objects in the classroom. Exchange ideas about their sound qualities: wood metal, plastic glass, etc. Discuss their **pitch** (high or low) and their **timbre** (quality of sound).
- Make some simple instruments from household objects. Include instruments played by blowing, twanging and scraping as well as by hitting and shaking.
- Sing some simple songs familiar to everyone. Use body movements to help recognise the **beat** — pat knees, tap or clap, snap fingers. Give individuals a chance to lead.
- Using finger and hand movements in the air, try to trace the **pitch** (up and down sounds) of a short and simple song you are all singing.
- Select a few short contrasted examples of music for listening. Initiate a discussion on the music heard, dealing with points such as the instruments, voices heard, the shape and mood of the music. Try to recall and imitate any short, clear fragments, rhythmic or melodic, from the music extract.

Note

- Read these, and other music activities of your own, to the National Curriculum ATs and PoS.
- Ask colleagues to contribute to general discussion on the value, music concepts involved, and performance problems encountered for each activity.
- Ensure staff go away with ideas for music with their class.
- Help teachers it adapt these activities for their own classes.
- Ask for suggestions of follow-up activities which would be useful for the next music meeting.

The staff can discuss what has been achieved during the INSET day, select ideas according to the children they teach, link with the National Curriculum Programmes of Study, and draw up a series of short lessons in music. At a later date a feedback session would be useful at which staff compare their teaching experiences, review music methods and materials and begin to construct a progressive framework for the whole-school's music. Ideally, the system of sharing music ideas and comparing results might be undertaken in conjunction with one or more local schools.

SPECIAL EDUCATIONAL NEEDS

It is vital to give every opportunity for pupils with special educational needs to have full access to experiences of National Curriculum Music. Encourage your colleagues to be positive about the musical abilities of all children, noting that music can be a unique source of individual achievement and personal satisfaction and a means of learning in other curricular fields.

It would be wise to request help from parents, specialist teachers and support staff in order to make special provision where needed. For example, musical material and instruments may require adaptations for pupils with hearing or sight problems. A computer with relevant software can be particularly useful, allowing pupils to compose with programmes that permit the formation and selection of musical material at the touch of a key.

Try to identify musically gifted children in your school. They will need special provision — instrumental lessons or wider resources - to allow them to develop their musical potential and interests. Their talents should be recognised and encouraged, giving them a sense of individual fulfilment and enabling them to make a full contribution to music in society.

FINAL NOTE

This chapter has shown that as music coordinator you will need to use all manner of resources, both human and material, in order to achieve a high standard of music in your school. Care in planning your work, allied to friendly discussion, with colleagues and an alert ear, will take you towards achieving the principal aim of teaching music: namely, the encouragement and development of children's understanding and enjoyment of music.

To summarise, how can you best develop music in your school? You might like to reflect on these points:

— look at the music needs of pupils and teachers;
— take stock of their present music experiences;
— in open discussion with colleagues come to an agreement on measures to be take and draw up a music planning scheme;
— as a whole staff, regularly scrutinise your school's music programme.

Ideally, your music scheme will be drawn up by yourselves for your own situation. However, there will probably be an increase in published music schemes especially produced for National Curriculum music. Basic information on these can be gathered from educational publishers, music suppliers and advertisements in music and education journals. You may be able to inspect some sample music schemes on approval from publishers, at a teachers' centre, resource centre or exhibition. Searching out another school which already uses a published scheme would be worthwhile; this gives you the chance to make an estimate founded on practical experience. Try to decide what you and your colleagues require from a published music course prior to examining what is available. No published material will entirely suit your own school. There is always a need for additional resources such as extra songs, cassettes, stories of composers and their music computer software. These could all be based in a central music resource point under your supervision.

We have tried to give some guidelines to prompt constructive thought about your coordinating role in the challenging years ahead. Effective curriculum, leadership in music depends largely on the coordinator. The role is an exacting one, but it is highly satisfying.

REFERENCES

Schools Council Working Paper 75: Primary, Schools' Council, London, 1983.

Music from 5 to 16, Curriculum Matters 4, HMSO, London, 1985.

National Curriculum Music Working Group: Interim Report, DES, London, 1990.

14

RELIGIOUS EDUCATION TODAY

This chapter aims to identify ways in which effective coordinators can enhance the religious education of children as a result of helping the whole staff to understand and implement the 1988 Education Reform Act (ERA) in relation to religious education. It outlines some major aspects of the role and suggests ways of handling them.

WHAT IS YOUR ROLE?

Your immediate task once (or preferably before), you have agreed to become the RE coordinator is establish the extent of your responsibilities. You are acting in the name of the headteacher, who clearly cannot carry curriculum responsibility across all subject areas, so he/she should have an important part of play in the definition to the role.

In many primary school RE and school worship are linked together. Indeed, some schools claims that their responsibilities for RE are entirely discharged within the school assembly. The 1988 ERA would not support this view.

Action Point 1

Arrange a meeting with your headteacher to discuss and agree the extent to the responsibilities you are undertaking.

Since the headteacher normally leads and organises assemblies, an RE coordinator need to establish at the outset and quite unambiguously, whether these are included or excluded from their brief.

One function of this brief should be to tell you to whom you are responsible. The task will prove more straightforward if it has the active support of the headteacher and other senior staff. A discussion of projected work plus progress reports should form a regular part of the coordinator's work. Clearly, these kinds of activities will take time. It is essential therefore to establish at the outset, the amount of time that will made available. Time and responsibilities go together and there is no point in agreeing to take on a role which will be impossible to fulfil.

Action point 2

Go through your diary and plan dates, one or two a term, at which you make a report to the headteacher.

Regular meetings between yourself and the head should be arranged. These will not usually be long, but will be a means of keeping the head formally aware of the work you are doing and provide a basis for discussion. The headteacher may also wish, on occasion, to take information to the governors. Reports may take the form of minutes of summaries of staff planning sessions which will show the progress of school policy writing. There may be suggestions for staff development sessions, requests for staff development sessions, requests for resources or ideas on ways of relating classroom RE to assemblies. Essentially their purpose is to keep RE from slipping out of sight in the welter of other school activities.

The third factor in this initial enquiry into the RE coordinator's role concerns time and resources. If you are to fulfil the coordinator's role satisfactorily, the school will need to provide you with:

- time to work alongside teachers in their classrooms;
- opportunities to attend in-service courses;
- time to prepare and present in-school training;
- time to edit the audit of RE materials within the school, to update and organise them.

You may find it useful to join with other coordinators to ensure that the finance for foundation subjects is adequate. Some schools may decide to decide to available money across the areas, whilst others may prefer to concentrate on one major area each year with smaller amounts fort the other subjects. If the guideline 'worst first' is adopted, RE should be very near the top of the list in most schools!

You will meet teachers who feel uncertain about the nature and content of RE. Apart from actual knowledge, there are concerns in many people's minds about faith-stances and indoctrination. These much be discussed and illuminated if progress is to be made. Such issues frequently emerge when possible content is discussed at a meeting. As Chair of such a discussion you will need to ensure that there is enough time to explore everyone's ideas in an open, low-key way. You are aiming to produce a policy that everyone will find acceptable.

Unlike the foundation areas, there have been RE syllabuses in existence since the early years of the century. All primary teachers should have followed the syllabus written or adopted by their LEA. Most of them consisted of selections of biblical teaching and were, to non-specialists teachers, repetitious and unhelpful. Consequently many teachers ignored them. However there have been significant changes recently in most syllabuses making them much more 'user-friendly'.

Part of your role, as coordinator, is to ensure that copies of the syllabus used by your LEA are available, form the basis of the school policy and are reflected in what goes on in classrooms. Church schools will also have the options of using the diocesan syllabus for RE instead of, or in conjunction with, the LEA document. The governing body is responsible for this decision. It would be sensible to know what has been decided before embarking on creating a school policy, or at least to keep the governors informed of your actions at each stage so that matters can be agreed simultaneously.

Action point 3

Face up to staff attitudes and beliefs you expect to meet. Write down those you think will be the most difficult to come to terms with. If possible discuss your fears with another RE coordinator and work out a strategy for coping with them.

RE has no SAT's not even any nationally imposed Programmes of Study. The variety of syllabuses in use would make the latter an impossibility. The danger is that insufficient time, attention and importance will be attached to learning in this area. One of your target should be change that.

Action 4

Ask your colleagues to help you by:

— *making an audit to all the RE materials in the school. It would be useful to put these under headings indicating whether they are for use by children or by teachers (don't forget the library stock).*

— *identifying what is currently used and what has only gathered dust for years.*

In recent years RE has frequently been seen as part of a theme or topic. In many cases it has sunk without trace because teachers have been unable to identify an RE stand in more specific terms than 'helping' or 'caring'. As coordinator, part of your role will be to sit beside teachers and look with them at their topic through on RE focus. Your own enhanced knowledge will enable you to suggest appropriate input of an implicit or explicit nature. Through discussion with individual you will also raise their awareness and lead them towards an ability to identify materials for themselves. This is another area where whole-staff discussions on school policy and programme should, in time, bear fruit.

WHAT YOU NEED TO KNOW

The Act

The basic requirements for RE and collective worship remain the same as stated in the 1944 Act. However the way in which the requirements are worked out in practice have changed in a number of ways. In this section we shall consider:

— the provisions of the 1988 Act relating to Religious Education and school worship;

— the nature of the Standing Advisory Council for Religious Education frequently referred to as SACRE;

— the Agreed Syllabus.

This description is of fan over-arching nature and does not attempt to enter into the fine detail of the Act. The coordinator will need access to a copy of the full section of the Act relating to Religious Education and collective worship. This is to be found in DES circular 3/89. *The Education Reform Act 1988: Religious Education and Collective Worship.* A copy of this document went to all schools.

Action point 5

Your school should have a copy of DES circular 3/89. Did it come to light in the audit? If not, is it lurking in the headteacher's room, somewhere? Find it and read it.

What does the 1988 Act say about Religious Education?

The title has been change from Religious Instruction to Religious Education. This reflects a very basic change in the approach to the subject from that of 1944.

These points remain the same

— There must be provision made for teaching RE to all pupils.

— In county schools it must be non-denominational and in accordance with a locally agreed syllabus.

— Parents have the right to withdraw their children from RE.

— Teachers have the same right of withdrawal from teaching RE as under the 1944 Act.

These points are different

— New Agree Syllabuses must , reflect the fact that religious traditions in this country are mainly Christian, whilst taking account of the teaching and practices of other major religions.

— RE must remain non-denominational in nature in country schools, but it is acceptable to teach about denominations.

— Every LEA must set up a Standing Advisory Council on Religious Education (SACRE).

— A SACRE may require an LEA to set up a conference to review a locally Agreed Syllabus.

The composition of such conferences may differ. This is discussed in the section on the locally Agreed Syllabus.

What does the Act say about collective worship?

These points remain the same

— There must be a daily act of collective worship and, in county schools, this must be not-denominational.

— Rights of withdrawal for pupils and teachers are upheld.

These are the changes

- There is more flexibility concerning timing and organisation of school worship: it can be at any time of day and it can provide separate acts of worship for pupils in different to teaching groups.
- Worship should be wholly or mainly of a broadly Christian character but, in county schools, not representative of any particular denomination.
- It is not necessary for every act of worship in a term to be of such a nature but the majority are required to be so.
- The headteacher, in consolation with the governing body, has the responsibility of deciding how acts of worship are best organised.
- Where the headteacher and governors feel that the above requirement are inappropriate to the background faiths of the pupils they may apply to the SACRE for 'a determination' to modify the acts of worship for some or all of the pupils.

What is a SACRE?

A SACRE (Standing Advisory Council on Religious Education) is now required to be set up by each LEA and will consist of four committees, one for each of the following interests:

- such Christian and other religious groups as will represent the local community;
- the Church of England;
- teacher associations;
- the LEA.

The SACRE's function is to advise the LEA on matters relating to RE and collective worship, in addition to which it has two specific functions:

1. This relates to the teaching of RE within the maintained schools. If it is felt that the syllabus is out of date the SACRE can require the LEA to review and amend it

2. This is linked to school worship. It is the SACRE which makes a judgement as to whether to grant school's applications to vary the balance of content in acts of worship. Woman LEAs use the SACRE as the forum for the consideration of complaints from parents, or others, on matters related to either of these areas.

Action point 6

Contact your LEA and ask for a list of the membership of the local SACRE and for a copy of any available reports.

The SACRE must publish a report on its work every year, which will mention all matters referred to it by the LEA with a summary of advice given in response. The report will also give an indication of any other areas in which the SACRE has advised the LEA during the year.

The Locally Agreed Syllabus

The LEA is required to identify a Locally Agreed Syllabus for use in county schools. They may either set up a conference to write a syllabus for their own authority or adopt the syllabus of another LEA. This is an LEA decision, not one made by individual schools. Where an LEA decides to set up a syllabus writing conference it must be made up from representatives from the groups constituting the SACRE.

When a syllabus has ben produced it must be agreed by the whole conference. It is then forward to the Secretary of State and will be enacted by Parliament. Thus, the Agreed Syllabus has the force of law. Since this is clearly a long, and expensive process, some of the more recent syllabuses have been produced in several sections. For example a statement of principles, aims, objectives and general framework form the legal document. This is supported by handbooks containing examples of themes and bibliographies which can be updated from time to time without going through the legal process on each occasion.

It will be clear, from the above, why there are no national Programmes of Study or SoAs in RE — each area has its own syllabus. The Act does permit an LEA to identify Programmes of Study and SoAs based on its own syllabus. There has been quite a lot of debate relating to the kinds of groupings of statements which would be appropriate. Some of these are outlined in publications such as *Attainment in RE — A Handbook for Teachers,* published by Westhill, and *Recognising*

Attainment in Religious Education from Essex LEA. The later publications intended to be used in connection with Essex LEA's own Agreed Syllabus but provides some interesting material for consideration in any school.

Action point 7

— *Have you now found copies of the Agreed Syllabus in current use in your LEA? If not, now is the time to get hold of some from the LEA.*

— *Buy one of the publications dealing with attainment in RE.*

— *Ask you local SACRE if they have produced or are producing any SoAs or Programmes of Study to accompany the current syllabus, or if there are any plans to revise or replace it.*

A number of examples and ideas are also given in the excellent Christian Education Movement (CEA) booklet *Planning RE in Schools* which would be valuable to any primary RE coordinator. As new syllabuses are produced, or existing ones revised, statements of attainment in terms of knowledge, skills and attitudes are being expressed. In the internal it would be perfectly possible to identify your own.

SHARING WITH COLLEAGUES

The overall aim of the RE coordinator should be to reach the point where:

— the place and purpose of RE as part of the children's educational experience is guaranteed to them and accepted by all the staff;

— there is a school policy for RE to which all teachers subscribe both in principal and in practice;

— there is an understanding of what is good practice in RE, a willingness to use a variety of approaches and an awareness of new ideas;

— the school can provide the resources, human and material, for the above.

How do you go about achieving this?

Action point 8

Go back to Chapter One and read through the list of points about communication. Apply them to your role.

And then softly, softly..............

Do not assume that any successful change will be a speedy process. People have all kinds of ideas about the nature of religion, which are unlikely to emerge at a first meeting and not at all if there is a feeling of rush and hurry about getting too may things done. However, you will also know how precious time is and how colleagues will rightly be resistant to meetings where they feel nothing is achieved. So, you need to proceed with caution:

- give adequate notice of meetings;
- prepare an agenda and publish it;
- identify times and stick to them — especially fishing times;
- produce briefing papers in good time to allow for informed discussion;
- prime colleagues who you want to make particular contributions, don't just drop on them but equally don't give the impression that outcome are already cut and dried.

Begin with something objective, such as *Action Point 3,* in which everyone can share. If this were done a short time before the meeting you could produce a master list for everyone. This would begin to focus people's minds on RE.

A CLEAR AND PURPOSEFUL FIRST MEETING

The first meeting should follow the outline suggested in Chapter One. In terms of RE this suggests that certain considerations should be included.

Where are we now ?

- As a whole school — do we have a school theme for any RE or for assemblies?
- In our classes — what kind of time, content and approaches are in use?

Where do we want to get to ?

— What does the Act say? Identify the major points of the Act related to RE, but do not go into unnecessary detail. Anyone could borrow Circular 3/89 and enjoy some riveting reading for themselves. However, you must make the point that RE and assembly are not the same thing. There must be time devoted to RE over and above the daily act of worship.

— What does the Agreed Syllabus say? (Only make passing mention at this point.)

— What is the educational purpose of RE?

— The DES booklet *Curriculum matters 2* (1998) quotes the aims of the overall curriculum as set out in the first section of the ERA. Maintained schools are required to provide.

— 'a balanced and based curriculum that,

(i) promotes the spiritual, moral, cultural, mental and physical development of pupils at the school and of society; and (ii) prepares such pupils for the opportunities, responsibilities and experiences of adult life.'

(Foreword)

Later in the booklet (paragraphs 78-81) there is some discussion of the nature of the spiritual dimension. We shall return to this later. HMI also outline what they consider to be appropriate elements of learning, identifying, knowledge, concepts, skills and attitudes. These elements provide the groupings under which many of the attempts to provide a Statement of Attainment for RE have been made.

It will be important to establish the educational nature of the subject in discussion which may arise at this point. In county schools there must be no question of teachers presenting any aspect of RE as material which pupils must accept personally, although it will be appropriate to explain that for members of particular faith groups, teaching and practices related to that faith will be part of the their beliefs and way of life.

— We need to provide to RE in line with the Act, the Agreed Syllabus and with educational purposes agreed amongst the staff.

How will we get there?

A series of targets with a realistic timescale is essential. This should not be so brief as to be impossible to complete — bearing in mind the claims of other subject areas and school responsibilities — not so long drawn out as to become tedious. Some intermediate targets and strategies are suggested in the next section. In a first meeting it would be valuable to negotiate some kind of written statement, however brief, from the staff which will form the basis of a commitment to continue and to agree the next meeting date (s).

TARGETS AND STRATEGIES

A school policy

One significant target will be to produce a working, well-resourced policy for RE. The needs of your school must be central. Although many schools will use the same Agreed Syllabus, their interpretation will be different and therefore no two school policies are likely to be identical.

You must take into account factors such as:

— The ethnic and cultural backgrounds represented in the school community.

— Links with faiths practised in homes.

— Facilities available locally which may be drawn upon to enhance children's awareness and experience e.g. temple, mosque, churches, synagogue, gurdwara.

— *The Curriculum from 5-16* (DES) which emphasises the need to introduce children to world faiths whether or not they are represented within the school. Some schools arrange 'twinning' patterns to overcome difficulties. How are you going to introduce work on world faiths into the curriculum? Have you had an opportunity to look at any of the appropriate schools programmes produced by Independent TV/BBC?

— The school(s) to which children will move for their next phase of education. Are there world faith links?

— The organisation of the curriculum generally, within your school. Consider your general distribution of class teaching/learning and individual work. How can RE fit into this?

— The various ways of integrating RE into curriculum, such as:

— a fully integrated theme where RE is given the same time as other subjects within the theme;

— a theme another subject is the central feature and RE is one of the peripheral ones;

— a theme where RE is the central but not the sole subject;

— a theme where RE is virtually the sole subjects under consideration.

Over the course of a year it would be usual for a planned balance between these approaches to the curriculum. There should certainly not only be themes where RE is on the periphery.

With all of these factors in mind and the Agreed Syllabus to hand, you are almost ready to begin to construct a policy. The other major conditioning factor relates to the concepts, attitudes and skills that you and your colleagues see as appropriate to the children within the school.

Take the principles, the major building blocks of your Agreed Syllabus, headings such as Human Questions, Celebrations, Religious Stories and Rituals and work out what general concepts, attitudes and skills come out of them. Do not worry at first about actual content. Think about your children. When you have done that, find the content which will enable you to develop the concepts, teach the skills, and foster the attitudes. This is where the syllabus will come into its own.

You will find it easier to begin with a programme for the early years classes and build up a pattern, rather than to try to produce work for all ages simultaneously. You can then mark where you:

1. introduce material;
2. revisit it, deepening, broadening and strengthening links.

This is what Bruner describes as the *spiral curriculum* and about which he says that any subject can be taught effectively in some intellectually honest way to any child at any stage of development. The spiral approach allows for both reinforcement and development, as based on their knowledge of the needs of individual children teachers can decide on the frequency of revisiting topics and concepts. As with any subject areas, the danger is that there will be repetition. It is important to structure the policy carefully so that this will be avoided and material differentiated sufficiently so that junior children will not presume that they have covered it before and consequently mentally 'switch off'.

Action point 9

Look at the Agreed Syllabus in the light of the school setting and needs and produce a framework for RE which would ensure progression not just repetition.

— Consider how much RE should be discrete and how much should be thematic and ensure a balance through each school year.

— Consider where faiths other than Christianity are to receive particular emphasis.

— Consider whether there should be come whole-school themes, and if so, what and where.

Ideally these should worked on in meetings of all the staff because this the best way to ensure that everyone will support the finished policy.

Evaluation

Your school policy will need to include means of evaluating the work done, in terms of assessing children' progress and development and promoting teacher self-evaluation.

Clearly some aspects of RE are more easily assessed that others. Some will remain within the subjective judgement of the teacher, but others are identifiable in terms of skills acquired, the understanding of concepts demonstrated and the increase in vocabulary. Teachers should be encouraged to evaluate their work in this area, as in any other, by reflecting on questions such as:

— How far did I achieve my intentions?

— What level of interest and attention was shown by the children?

— In what directions have I extended knowledge, taught or development skills, and provided opportunity for reflection and open discussion?

There is useful section on assessment in the CEM booklet, *Planning RE in Schools.*

Staff development

Alongside this evaluation, teachers will need to look at a variety of approaches to RE and, together, identify areas where staff development in needed, such as information about other faiths and ideas for celebrating festivals. Various ways in which staff can reflect upon their needs are outlined in Chapter One. A number of these are particularly appropriate to RE. You might decide to invite one or a series of people into school to speak to staff. For instance, someone from the local SACRE should be able to give a general overview of its work and possibly provide information relating to syllabus and SoAs which are being produced. You might want to find speakers from some of the major faiths who would be prepared to provide general background, or talk about specific aspects such as festivals or rites of passage. In some schools there will be parents who might be approached either to do this or put you in touch with religious community leaders. Alternatively, the SACRE should be able to provide contact names.

The same kind of process might be followed if you decided that a visit to a place of worship would be a suitable staff activity for a training day.

Local libraries may also have lists of places of worship and/or religious leaders and may be able to provide topic boxes of reference books for staff use. Some libraries have video lending sections which would provide appropriate audit background materials. Local authority advisors, knowledgeable colleagues from other school or members of staff from HE institutions are other possible sources of input. Look out for short courses or single meetings provided by LEAs which relate to RE. Once again, the local SACRE may hold this kind of information or, indeed, may set up meetings from time to time.

RESOURCES

Most primary teachers have, or develop, the hoarding instinct and this will certainly be valuable to you in setting up an RE resources centre. This is most usefully done in conjunction with your developing RE policy. There is a strong impetus to provide the resources when their use is enshrined in an official school document. There should also be some kind of balance between artefacts and books.

There are various ways of setting about building up resources—you must decide which suits your circumstances best. Offered below is simply one way — some ideas to start you off. However, I would urge you most strongly to use some of your precious resources to subscribe to a publication such as the Christian Education Movement Primary Mailing (details in bibliography). This is issued once a term and includes a magazine with up-to-date information about what is going on in the world of RE, details of new books and materials including reviews, notification of courses, background information on a variety of aspects of RE and DIY ideas for resources. Each term, a booklet is included with content suggestions relating to a theme for the whole primary age range and some ideas for worship. Over a period of time these build into a very valuable staff resource.

Action point 10

Review your existing materials. Do not be afraid to discard the rubbish. Old tattered books or pictures will not motivate children in positive ways, nor will copies of the Bible that need a magnifying glass in order to read them. Sometimes individual pages of books can be saved to make into work cards or information cards, or pictures re-mounted — but be rigorous. Keep a lookout for sloppy pictures!

List what you need to add and divide it into priority sections e.g. Immediate, Soon, Later, (unless someone has left you a fortune of course!) Finally, decide how your materials will be grouped and stored. This is really important, otherwise your materials will be spread around the school so that no one can find anything when they want it. Good storage, even if you have to begin with a series of stout cardboard boxes, will keep things accessible and in good condition.

You must then decide what you want to collect for each of the world faiths you are going to consider. These could include stories, pictures, posters, background information, words and music, artefacts, recipes, audio cassettes, and video cassettes. For instance:

Christianity: materials related to Christmas, Easter, Pentecost;

Judaism: Passover, Succot, Channukah;

Islam: Eid-ul-Fitr, Eid-ul-Adha, Ramadan, Hajj;

Hinduism: Divali, Holi;

and other faith or celebrations decided upon by the school, such as the Chinese New Year.

Materials of all faiths related to *birth, initiation, marriage, days/ places of worship, materials used in worship.*

As an example, here are some suggested collections for Christianity:

In the ***Easter Box***

The Easter story, plan crosses, idea for setting up a display with eggs, hot cross buns, Easter cards, songs, poems. Prints of some of the great pictures relating to Easter. Background information about any of these. Information about any of these. Information about how people in different Christian groups in various parts of the world celebrate Easter.

In the ***Christian Worship Box***

Different kinds of crosses — actual or pictures. Pictures of different churches and ideas on what to look for on a church visit. Prayer books, hymn books, copies of the scriptures, rosaries, holy pictures, postcards showing stained glass windows, instruction for making these from tissue paper, varieties of candles.

I am sure that, even as you read this, you will have ideas of your own and be saying 'Oh yes and....' You then need to think about how you will collect all these things. Clearly, you could buy them all. Probably you will have to buy some of them. There may, however, be staff or parents who will be prepared to give things that they have at home but no longer use. You will have to assure them that everything will be treated with appropriate respect and handled carefully. It is sometimes possible to find a travel agent who will donate large posters of some of the holy places of various faiths.

Staff or parents on foreign holiday may be able to buy religious artefacts much more cheaply than you could buy them here, if they know what you are looking for. It is very much a matter of collecting things over a period of time and looking after them.

You will also need to buy books that children can use and decide where these are best kept. Many of the library service will provide boxes of materials on loan which could be used, for example, during a whole-school theme. Another possibility would be to invite people from faith groups into school to show precious things to a class or age group and talk about them.

Resources are vital — especially things that children can see, small, touch, as well as pictures — and it is a very good way of teaching respect for things which are precious to other people, if not to yourself

As RE coordinator, you are probably wondering what on earth you have taken on, or mentally rehearsing your reasons for being unable, after all, to accept this role. Take heart. There are ways of getting help and it is an important job. Build up your contact — SACRE, local religious leaders, LEA advisors and advisory teachers, HE establishments. Build up your resources, use the bibliography for some initial suggestions, plus information from short television programmes, Sunday newspaper supplements. Encourage colleagues to collect as well. Aim at steady, not spectacular progress — and you will surprise yourself.

